Gluten-Free
Cookies

Jeanne Basye

Gluten-Free Cookies

Copyright 2008 by Jeanne Basye
First limited edition

Printed and bound in the United States of America. All rights reserved. No part of this book may be reproduced in any form or by any electronic or mechanical means including information storage and retrieval systems without prior permission in writing from the author, except a reviewer, who may quote brief passages in a review.

The photographs in this book are the sole property of the author and are not to be copied or distributed in any format without the written permission of the author. Exception: clip art photos (pages 11, 14, 29, 62, 94, 108, 147, 150, 159).

Published by What No Wheat Enterprises
4757 East Greenway Road
Suite 107 B-91
Phoenix, AZ 85032
Website: www.whatnowheat.com

Interior design, layout and index: Lisa Liddy, The Printed Page, www.theprintedpage.com
Food Stylist: Harriett Granthen, Granthen Studios®, Phoenix, AZ, granthenstudios@mindspring.com
Photographer: Curt Granthen, Granthen Studios®, Phoenix, AZ, granthenstudios@mindspring.com
Cover design: Curt Granthen and Lisa Liddy
Printed by: Bang Printing, Brainerd, MN, www.bangprinting.com

ISBN: 978-0-9724154-4-6

The information in this book is for educational purposes only. It is not intended to replace the advice of a physician or medical practitioner. Do not start a totally gluten-free diet without seeking medical assistance. The publisher and author are not responsible for any errors, omissions or misstatements that may exist within this publication. This publication is not to be construed as the whole or entire information on the subject of baking, ingredients, processes or any of the medical conditions or personal choices associated with a gluten-free diet. At the time of this writing, products listed were gluten-free. Always read food labels.

For additional books: contact What No Wheat Enterprises at www.whatnowheat.com

Front cover pictures: In the front, left to right: Peanut Butter Cookies (p. 18), Chocolate Chip Cookies (p. 15), Sugar Cookies (p. 23). Back cover cookie pictures, see pages 46 and 106.

All net proceeds from the sale of this book benefit national celiac support organizations and education.

Dedication

For Jack, Matt, Jason and Morgenne
who sweeten my life

and

In honor of my mom and in memory of my dad
for being my best life teachers

Acknowledgments

To love and share your time and talents with others is the essence of life. My life has been blessed with many kind and generous people who have shared their time and unique talents to bring this book to fruition.

Thank you:
Harriett Granthen, food stylist
Curt Granthen, food photographer
Lisa Liddy, book designer
Chris Kurtzman, printer
Paula LaFon, computer and technical advisor
Cathie Shivey, manuscript editor
Keith Weiskamp, book advisor
Elaine Blossom Nichols, color advisor
Collin Stone, cookie logo designer
LynnRae Ries, mentor

And numerous taste testers, ages 2 to 92 years, who evaluated and approved all my cookies

Many thanks to recipe contributors:
Kathy Griesbacher—-Chocolate Macaroons
Margie Molittieri—Walnut Chocolate Chip Biscotti

Special thanks to my family and friends for their encouragement, support and love throughout this cookie adventure.

Heartfelt gratitude and love to my husband, Jack, for giving me perspective and making it all worthwhile. You are the best!

Finally and most importantly, I thank God for all my blessings and the extraordinary people He has put in my life. His love is never ending!

—Jeanne Basye

Contents

I am...The Gluten-Free Cookie Lady 1

Cookie-Baking FUNdamentals 3
Great Gluten-Free Flour Mixture 4
Proper Baking Equipment 6
Quality Ingredients 8
Accurate Baking Measurements 9
Proper Mixing Techniques 9
Accurate Temperatures 10
Accurate Baking Times 10
Proper Cooling 10
Proper Storage 10

Gluten-Free Cookie Recipes 11
All-Time Classic Favorites 13
Best-Ever Bars and Brownies 25
Chocolate-Lover Cookies 47
Fabulous Fruity 'n Spicy Cookies 61
Naturally Nutty Cookies 79
No-Bake, No-Fuss Cookies 93
Peanut Butterlicious Cookies 107

Beyond Cookies 119
All About Nuts 121
Flavored Scented Sugars & More 129
Sweet Fillings 133
Fantastic Frostings & Glazes 141

Bonus Recipes 147
Fabulous Waffles 148
Great Granola 149
Jack's Homemade Vanilla Ice Cream 150

Techniques 151
Top Ten Cookie-Baking Tricks 152
Equivalent Charts 154
Cookie Troubleshooting Guide 155

Resources 159
National Celiac Support Organizations & More. 161
Gluten-Free Baking Products 162
Specialty Items 164

Index 165

I am...The Gluten-Free Cookie Lady

In our household any celebration or event was cookie time. As a child, I loved to help my mom bake cookies because I could lick the beaters, eat the dough and decorate the cookies. I always enjoyed the smell and anticipation of eating the cookies right out of the oven. Baking cookies was fun, easy and rewarding!

When I was 10 years old, I entered sugar cookies at the Woodbury County Fair in Moville, Iowa. My first solo attempt turned out cookies that fell apart. In going over the recipe with my mom, we discovered I had forgotten to add the eggs to make them stick together. That was my first lesson in following directions. My next attempt won a blue-ribbon at the fair. Since that time, I have been fascinated by the baking process and have enjoyed years of cookie baking, cookie gift-giving and cookie recipe collection.

Throughout the years, sharing freshly baked home-made cookies with family and friends has been a fun part of my life. Everyone in my family loves cookies, especially my husband, Jack. But in 2002, cookie baking as I had known it changed forever when Jack was diagnosed with dermatitis herpetiformis (a form of celiac disease) and we made the decision to become a gluten-free household (no wheat, rye, barley or cross-contaminated oats) to combat his disease. My emphasis became gluten-free.

I started searching for gluten-free cookies but found most of the store-bought ones dry, tasteless and expensive. At the same time, we joined a celiac support group and discovered someone was starting a Gluten-Free Cooking School. I signed up for classes and soon was experimenting and creating gluten-free cookie recipes. I would bake gluten-free cookies and bring them to the cooking class for class members to taste and evaluate. Each time their reactions were overwhelmingly positive. Class attendees requested my recipes and always wanted to take any leftover cookies home. Encouraged, I was challenged to create more gluten-free cookies.

By 2003, I had formulated my own nutritious gluten-free flour mixture. I was asked to teach cookie classes at the Gluten-Free Cooking Club/School and write a cookie column for their newsletter. Renewed vigor and commitment came in 2005, when all three of my adult step-children, Matt, Jason and Morgenne, were diagnosed with celiac disease. My mission became more personal and meaningful. Gluten-free cookies became my passion.

Being retired, I had the time, desire and motivation to create the best gluten-free cookies, and that was my goal. I turned my kitchen into a gluten-free laboratory and found many of my neighbors, friends and even strangers (over 200 people) to be willing cookie taste testers and evaluators. Each morning, neighbors lined up at my door asking what new gluten-free cookie I was creating that day! I became "The Gluten-Free Cookie Lady." They couldn't believe these cookies were gluten-free because they tasted as good as or better than "regular" cookies. Requests for my cookie recipes increased and inquiries for a gluten-free cookie cookbook began.

So I embarked on the greatest cookie adventure of all: to write this gluten-free cookie cookbook and share my recipes with you. All of my 150 cookie creations were evaluated for taste, texture and appearance. The best were labeled keepers and considered for my cookbook. Besides the "best of the best" cookies recipes and embellishments, I am sharing tips and information I learned along the way that will make your baking experience easier, more rewarding and earn you cookie kudos.

Gluten-free cookies are the sweetest gift there is. I hope you have **FUN** baking my gluten-free cookies and enjoy sharing them with others. With a little effort, you'll receive big rewards. May your cookie jar always be full!

Jeanne Basye, The Gluten-Free Cookie Lady

For those unfamiliar with Celiac Disease, here is a short introduction. For more information, see Resources on page 159.

According to Peter Green, M.D., and other recognized medical leaders in the field, celiac disease is a genetic, autoimmune disorder affecting children and adults. Those with celiac disease (CD) cannot eat foods that contain gluten, a protein found in wheat, barley, rye and their derivatives. In people with CD, gluten triggers an autoimmune response and the body attacks itself, destroying healthy tissue, such as intestinal tissue. This, in turn, interferes with the small intestine's ability to absorb nutrients from food, which may lead to malnutrition and a host of other complications.

There are no drugs to treat celiac disease and there is no cure. The only effective treatment, according to medical experts in the field and national celiac support organizations, is a lifelong commitment to a strict gluten-free diet. This means avoiding all forms of **wheat** (including bulgur, couscous, durum, einkorn, emmer, faro, graham, kamut, matza, matzo, matzah, seitan, semolina, and spelt also called dinkle) and related grains: **barley**, **rye** and **triticale**. Current research has shown that most people who are gluten-free can consume oats that have not been cross-contaminated with the forbidden grains. Consuming gluten-free oats (also called pure, uncontaminated oats) is a personal decision. **Note:** Gluten-Free always means wheat-free. However, products labeled Wheat-Free are not necessarily gluten-free. They may contain other forbidden grains. Always read labels.

Cookie-Baking FUNdamentals

What makes a great gluten-free cookie? First you must start with wonderful cookie recipes (you already have them in this cookbook!). Then you must understand gluten-free cookie baking **FUN**damentals. After that, you can bake award-winning gluten-free cookies that everyone will rave about and love to eat.

Look inside and find the essential cookie-baking **FUN**damentals.

Great Gluten-Free Flour Mixture 4
Proper Baking Equipment. 6
Quality Ingredients 8
Accurate Baking Measurements 9
Proper Mixing Techniques 9
Accurate Temperatures. 10
Accurate Baking Times 10
Proper Cooling 10
Proper Storage 10

Great Gluten-Free Flour Mixture

On a gluten-free diet all forms of **wheat** (including bulgur, couscous, durum, einkorn, emmer, faro, graham, kamut, matza, matzo, matzah, seitan, semolina, and spelt also called dinkle), and related grains: **barley, rye and triticale** are the forbidden grains. Current research has shown that most people who are gluten intolerant can consume pure, uncontaminated (gluten-free) oats.

Therefore, the most important ingredient and the one that makes gluten-free cookies different is the flour. Gluten-free flours affect both the structure and taste of the cookie. Unlike baking with wheat flour, there is no single gluten-free flour that can be used alone for successful baked goods. Rather, gluten-free baking requires a combination of alternative flours and xanthan gum to produce the same quality results.

The Gluten-Free Cookie Lady's Flour fits the bill to a tee. It is the signature flour mixture that I developed to add more flavor, fiber and nutrition to the cookies and has become the hallmark of my cookie recipes. Once you make the flour mixture, it is easy to make everything in this cookbook and more. Xanthan gum, an important ingredient in gluten-free baking, is not part of my flour formula. It is added separately to each cookie recipe. Find it in health food stores.

Make a big batch of flour mixture, label and date the container, store it in the refrigerator or freezer and have it ready when needed. Then all you need to do is bring the flour mixture to room temperature before using, add xanthan gum as recipe directs and voilá—fabulous baked goods.

The Gluten-Free Cookie Lady's Flour Formula

INGREDIENTS	Makes 4 ¼ cups	Makes 8½ cups	Makes 12¾ cups	Makes 17 cups
Brown Rice Flour	1½ cups	3 cups	4½ cups	6 cups
Sweet Rice Flour	¾ cup	1½ cups	2¼ cups	3 cups
Tapioca Starch	⅔ cup	1 ⅓ cups	2 cups	2⅔ cups
Cornstarch	⅓ cup	⅔ cup	1 cup	1⅓ cups
Navy Bean Flour	¼ cup	½ cup	¾ cup	1 cup
Almond Flour (Meal)	¼ cup	½ cup	¾ cup	1 cup
Sorghum Flour	¼ cup	½ cup	¾ cup	1 cup
Potato Starch (not flour)	¼ cup	½ cup	¾ cup	1 cup

While the cookie recipes are made with this flour mixture, other gluten-free flour mixtures may be used with successful results. I recommend you try my flour mixture first, then experiment with others. Compare the taste, texture and nutrient value; then decide.

For similar results, use a gluten-free flour mix that does not include xanthan gum; then follow recipe. Some commercial gluten-free flour mixes contain xanthan gum; adjustments may be needed.

The Gluten-Free Cookie Lady's Flour Ingredients

The chart below describes the flours and starches used in the **The Gluten-Free Cookie Lady's Flour** and suggestions for locating the products.

Ingredient/Description/Substitution	Where to Buy
Almond Flour: Also called almond meal. Made from whole, raw and unsalted almonds, it is high in protein, fiber, iron, magnesium, calcium, vitamin E and other nutrients. *For those allergic to nuts, substitute with sorghum flour in equal amounts.* Make your own flour by grinding whole raw almonds in food processor until finely ground. If needed, add 1 to 2 teaspoons of sugar to prevent paste-like texture.	Health food stores or some supermarkets (Resources page 162)
Brown Rice Flour: Milled from unpolished brown rice, it contains bran and is high in magnesium, phosphorous and potassium. Buy the <u>finest ground</u> to avoid the grainy texture rice flour imparts.	Health food stores or some supermarkets (Resources page 162)
Cornstarch: A refined starch made from corn, it provides a light and tender texture to baked goods. *For those allergic to corn, substitute with tapioca starch in equal amounts.*	Supermarkets
Navy Bean Flour: Derived from whole navy beans, it lacks the strong "bean" taste found in other bean flours. It is high in complex carbohydrates, protein and dietary fiber, low in fat, calories and sodium. The brand I use is called Heartland's Finest.	Some health food stores or call Heartland's Finest for nearest distributors. (Resources page 163)
Potato Starch: Also called potato starch flour or potato powder (Asian markets), it is a fine white starch made from grinding dried potatoes and provides a light, airy texture to baked goods. **Potato Flour is not potato starch** and can not be substituted for it.	Asian markets, health food stores or some supermarkets in the ethnic aisle (Resources page 162)
Sorghum Flour: Also called milo or jowar, it has a mild, sweet flavor much like the flavor of wheat and complements other gluten-free flours. It is a powerhouse of nutrition in protein and dietary fiber.	Health food stores, Indian markets or some supermarkets (Resources page 162)
Sweet Rice Flour: Also known as sticky rice flour, waxy rice flour or glutinous rice flour (glutinous refers to sticky texture). It is starchier and smoother in texture than other rice flours and has a sweet sticky consistency. It helps bind ingredients together and keeps baked goods moist and tender.	Asian markets, health food stores or some supermarkets in the Oriental aisle (Resources page 162)
Tapioca Starch: Also called tapioca starch flour, tapioca flour, cassava, manioc, or yucca. Made from the root of tropical cassava plant, it is light, velvety and bland. It adds chewiness and elasticity to baked goods.	Asian markets, Latin American markets (cassava flour), health food stores or some supermarkets (Resources page 162)

Proper Baking Equipment

The type and quality of equipment are as important as the balance of ingredients and techniques. The proper equipment makes the whole baking process more efficient and convenient. Consider these examples:

- Using a **wire mesh strainer** to combine all dry ingredients is essential in gluten-free baking because it removes lumps, aerates the flours and incorporates leavenings, spices, salt and xanthan gum into a homogenous mix before adding to wet ingredients. Dry ingredients are evenly distributed in the dough and overmixing is reduced.

- Using a **free-standing oven thermometer** (placed on the center rack in the center of the oven) verifies that the oven temperature registers correctly and prevents unpredictable and undesirable baking results. A too-hot oven will crisp the exterior of a cookie too quickly, preventing it from spreading and leaving the inside underdone. A too-low oven temperature can result in dried-out cookies or ones that don't rise or spread properly. Before placing cookies in the oven, check and adjust the heat if necessary. Oven temperature must be accurate to ensure baking success.

- Using a **food processor** aids in making almond flour which saves money and time.

- Using a **free-standing heavy-duty mixer fitted with a paddle attachment** allows you to mix the ingredients while doing something else.

- Using a **cookie scoop** with a spring-release mechanism helps to make uniform-size cookies. It is easy to dip the cookie scoop into the dough, scrape excess off the side of the mixing bowl and drop onto cookie sheet. Cookies bake evenly because they are the same size. Cookie scoops come in several sizes and are found in kitchen specialty stores. I use either a 1½ or 2 tablespoon cookie scoop to make cookies the easy and fast way.

- Lining cookie sheets with **parchment paper** helps cookies retain their shape, bake evenly, prevents overbrowning, ensures easy removal and reduces cleanup time. It may be reused for numerous batches of cookies.

- Lining the bottom and sides of a baking pan with **non-stick aluminum foil**, such as Reynolds® Wrap Release®, ensures easy removal of bars and ease of cutting.

- Using a **timer** helps to ensure cookies are removed from the oven at exactly the right time. An extra one or two minutes in the oven can result in overbaked or burnt cookies. Most ovens are already fitted with a timer, but if you do not have an oven with a timer, it is well worth investing in one.

- Buying **high quality baking/cookie sheets** can last you a lifetime. Light-colored, dull finished, heavy gauge aluminum, one-sided (my preference) cookie sheets are the most durable and best as they allow better air movement around the cookies and more even baking results. They won't buckle in high temperatures, distort the shape of your cookies or develop hot-spots, which might cause burning. Purchase cookie sheets at least two inches narrower and shorter than your oven to ensure proper heat distribution while baking.

- Using **wire cooling racks** with small rectangular grids provide better support for cooling cookies and smaller cookies are less likely to slip through the grids.

Recommended Baking Equipment

#1 Bench (dough) scraper
#2 Cookie spatula
#3 Offset spatula
#4 Microplane® Grater
#5 Spring-released cookie scoop
#6 Measuring spoons
#7 Free-standing mixer with paddle attachment
#8 Dry measuring cups
#9 Liquid measuring cups
#10 Wire mesh strainer
#11 Parchment paper and non-stick aluminum foil
#12 Small grid cooling rack
#13 Cookie sheets
#14 Baking pan (8 x 8 x 2-inch)
#15 Potholders

Not pictured:
Food processor
Oven thermometer

Quality Ingredients

The recipe is only as good as the ingredients. In other words, you can't expect a championship cookie using second-rate ingredients. Using pure extracts, good chocolate, fresh nuts and spices and a flavorful, well-balanced gluten-free flour mix will take your cookie from average to outstanding.

Cookie ingredients are divided into five categories: **strengtheners, tenderizers, chemical leavening agents, flavors** and **extras**. Here is a short lesson on ingredients and their contribution to the baked cookie.

Strengtheners
Strengtheners provide structure, texture and flavor to cookies. Gluten-free flours, milk products, whole eggs, egg whites and xanthan gum are strengtheners which hold the cookie together. Using a good gluten-free flour mix such as **The Gluten-Free Cookie Lady's Flour** can make all the difference in the quality, texture and taste of the cookie. **Xanthan gum** is a crucial ingredient in gluten-free baking because it replaces the gluten found in wheat. Without it, cookies tend to lack texture and structure, and will crumble.

Tenderizers
Tenderizers provide tenderness, flavor, moistness, sweetness, texture and color to cookies. Fats, sugars, egg yolks and acids such as lemon juice are tenderizers. Fats (unsalted butter, vegetable oil, shortening and nut butters) and sweeteners (granulated or superfine sugars, light or dark brown sugar, confectioners' sugar also called powdered sugar, honey, molasses, maple syrup, and corn syrup) contribute unique characteristics to the cookie, and change the taste, flavor and texture of a cookie.

Unsalted butter provides unparalleled flavor; it is superior to salted butter because it has a sweeter, fresher and cleaner flavor. In comparison, a cookie made with vegetable shortening is more likely to retain its shape and is less likely to spread but lacks flavor. Cookies made with honey have a softer more chewy consistency. Ones made with confectioners' sugar have a tight velvety crumb and those made with brown sugar produce a moister cookie than ones made with granulated sugar.

Egg yolks provide a tender texture, while egg whites (strengthener) have a drying effect in cookies.

Chemical Leavening Agents
Chemical Leavening Agents contribute color, texture and volume to cookies. Baking powder, baking soda and cream of tartar are the leavening agents used in cookies. Baking powder (acid) produces lighter-colored, soft, puffier cookies. Baking soda (alkaline) neutralizes acidic ingredients (buttermilk, honey, citrus, molasses, cocoa powder, chocolate, etc.) and makes cookies spread and brown more. Many recipes have both baking powder and baking soda to ensure even browning and a fine texture. Cream of tartar (acid) is a component of baking powder. It is sometimes used in combination with baking soda as a leavening agent in cookies or used to stabilize beaten egg whites.

Flavors
Flavors give dimension, taste and color to cookies. Flavors can be sweet, sour, bitter or salty. Salt, pure extracts, spices, herbs, citrus zest, cocoa and dry pudding mixes are examples of flavor. Intensify taste by combining and layering flavors such as using lemon dry pudding mix, lemon zest and lemon oil in the dough and topping the cookie with a lemon glaze. This combination produces a sweet and tangy taste in the cookie. A little bit of salt rounds out other flavors and prevents the cookies from tasting "flat."

Extras
Extras enhance the cookie's taste. Extras impart visual beauty, contribute flavor, and add texture and nutritional value to the cookies. Nuts, peanuts, seeds (poppy, sesame or pumpkin seeds) and gluten-free cereals add nutritional value and crunchiness. Dried fruit and jams provide nutritional value, chewiness and sweetness. Chocolate, marshmallows, coconut, assorted of gluten-free candies and flavored gluten-free chips furnish extra sweetness.

Accurate Baking Measurements

Measuring ingredients accurately with the appropriate measuring tools means you'll get consistent results every time you make a cookie recipe. Accurate measurements can make the difference between yummy and yucky. For example, too much gluten-free flour can cause dry, tough cookies and too little can cause flat, pancake-like cookies.

Always use dry-ingredient cups to measure dry ingredients and liquid-measuring cups (glass ones with a spout) to measure liquid ingredients; the two kinds of cups do not hold the same volume. Make sure the cups for dry measure have straight rims for leveling off ingredients. Read liquid measurements by placing cup on counter and bending down so that your eyes are in line with the marks on the cup. Always use standard graduated measuring spoons (not a regular spoon) to measure both liquid and dry ingredients.

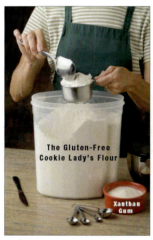

Before measuring, stir flour to aerate. Use spoon to fill measuring cup. Don't dip, pack or shake measuring cup or inaccurate measurement may result.

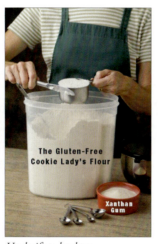

Use knife to level top.

Pass flour and all dry ingredients through wire mesh sieve.

Some almond flour will remain in sieve; put it in bowl. Stir dry ingredients again to ensure better blending and absorption of other ingredients.

Proper Mixing Techniques

Mixing methods, among other factors, influence the texture (light and tender, soft and chewy, crisp, or dense) of the cookie. The purpose of mixing is to incorporate the ingredients in a homogenous manner. Mixing techniques used in this book include: beating, stirring and food processing. Each method gives a different texture and character to the cookie. For example, cookies made with minimal or no beating bake denser and may have a chewy texture (brownies), while cookies made with extended beating (4 minutes) produces a light and tender cookie (sugar cookies).

Accurate Temperatures

Bring all ingredients (unsalted butter, eggs, milk, etc.) to **room temperature** to form a smooth homogenous mixture and a better cookie texture.

Baking at the correct **oven temperature** is crucial to the success of your recipe. Never begin baking in an oven that has not been brought up to the temperature specified in the recipe. It takes 15 to 20 minutes to preheat an oven (don't rely on the oven's built-in preheat indicator). This step should never be overlooked because it can literally make the difference between your recipe succeeding or failing. Incorrect baking temperatures, whether too high or too low, can ruin the taste and texture of cookies. Purchase a free-standing oven thermometer to ensure accurate oven temperature.

Accurate Baking Times

Check cookie doneness at the minimal baking time suggested. Other variables such as altitude, humidity or individual ovens contribute to baking time and must be adjusted accordingly. Every oven and every kitchen bakes a little differently. Bake one "test" cookie as a sample to gauge correct baking time for your oven, humidity or altitude conditions. Then adjustments can be made without ruining the entire batch of cookies. It is generally better to slightly underbake rather than to overbake gluten-free cookies. Cookies continue to bake on the cookie sheet after they are removed from the oven.

Proper Cooling

Use wire racks with small grids to cool cookies. The rack allows air to flow around the cookies and prevents them from becoming soggy. Some cookies need a longer time to set before being transferred to wire racks to cool completely. Follow the recipe's directions.

Cool the cookie sheet completely before placing the next batch of dough on it. A hot sheet will cause dough to melt prematurely. This may cause overspreading, deformed looking cookies, or alter the baking time. Use two cookie sheets. While one baking sheet is in the oven put the other one in refrigerator to cool. Keep alternating sheets in this fashion until cookies are all baked.

Proper Storage

Gluten-free cookies are best stored in airtight containers up to 2-3 days or frozen up to 2 months. Follow the storage directions specified in the recipe. Be sure to store similar cookies together. For example, crisp and soft cookies need to be stored in separate containers or the soft ones will soften the crisp cookies. Cookies with strong flavors such as peppermint can permeate other cookies. To prevent soft cookies from drying out, add an apple or orange to the container. If crisp cookies turn soft, pop them into a 300°F. oven for 3 to 5 minutes.

Gluten-Free Cookie Recipes

Let's go to the kitchen!

All-Time Classic Favorites

What makes homemade cookies so irresistible? Could it be their smell, taste and texture that tug at our heartstrings! And what makes a cookie "classic"? When I polled people, their top cookies were: Chocolate Chip, Sugar Cookies, Oatmeal-Raisin, Peanut Butter and Snickerdoodles.

Look inside to find these cookie classics- now made gluten-free. I bet no one can tell they are gluten-free! In fact, testers said these cookies are better than their wheat counterpart. Hope you'll agree.

- Chocolate Chip Cookies 15
- Magical Macaroons 16
- Oatmeal-Raisin Cookies 17
- Peanut Butter Cookies 18
- PB & Oatmeal-Raisin Chipsters 19
- Snickerdoodles 20
- Spicy Molasses Cookies 21
- Spritz Cookies 22
- Sugar Cookies 23

Clockwise from upper left: Spicy Molasses Cookies (p. 21), Peanut Butter Cookies (p. 18), Chocolate Chip Cookies (p. 15), Snickerdoodles (p. 20), and Magical Macaroons (p. 16).

All-Time Classic Know-How:

Bring ingredients to room temperature quickly by the following methods:

▲ Place eggs in bowl of very warm water for 5 to 7 minutes.

▲ Cut butter in small pieces and let stand for 5 to 7 minutes.

▲ Place liquids in microwave and heat for 15 to 20 seconds.

Some say salt, a preservative, is added to butter to hide inferior quality. Use unsalted butter for best results.

"Grade" of egg is a measurement of quality. Grade AA is the highest quality and Grade A is next highest quality. Shell color is based on the breed of the hen and has nothing to do with an egg's quality, flavor or nutrients. Brown shell or white, both are good. Use large eggs.

Store eggs in their carton—shells are porous and can absorb refrigerator odors.

Do not freeze cookie dough made with <u>whipped</u> egg whites because the egg whites break down during freezing and cookies may not bake properly.

Many bakers prefer using Rumford® baking powder because it's the only one that doesn't contain an aluminum compound (sodium aluminum sulfate) which may give baked goods a bitter aftertaste. Find the Rumford brand in the baking aisle of most supermarkets.

Solid vegetable shortening such as Crisco® comes conveniently packaged in sticks marked with tablespoon and cup measurements. In 2007, Crisco shortening products were reformulated to contain no trans fat while maintaining 50 percent less saturated fat than butter. Two varieties are available: Traditional All-Vegetable and Butter Flavor. Find in the baking aisle at supermarkets.

For Best Results:

■ Read entire recipe to ensure necessary ingredients and equipment are on hand or if any advance procedure needs to be done.

■ Have **all** ingredients at room temperature. Use quality ingredients.

■ Preheat the oven at least 15 minutes. Keep ovenproof thermometer inside oven to ensure accurate temperature.

■ Measure accurately and mix according to directions. Scrape bowl often to ensure homogenous dough.

■ Use spring-release cookie scoop for uniform size that bakes evenly and at same time.

■ Bake one cookie sheet at a time on the middle rack of the oven. Use quality cookie sheets.

■ Check cookies at the minimum baking time; continue baking, if necessary, in one-minute intervals. Every oven bakes a little differently. Bake one "test" cookie to gauge baking time in **your** oven. Better to underbake than overbake.

Chocolate Chip Cookies

Want an easy-to-make, thick and chewy chocolate chip cookie? Make this one for an ultimate treat. (Photo page 12)

2¼ cups The GF Cookie Lady's Flour (page 4)   1 teaspoon xanthan gum   1 teaspoon baking soda   ½ teaspoon salt
½ cup (1 stick) unsalted butter, melted and cooled   ⅔ cup firmly packed dark brown sugar   ⅔ cup granulated sugar   1 teaspoon pure vanilla extract   1 teaspoon pure almond extract
2 large eggs
1½ cups semisweet chocolate chips

Cookie Tip:

 The quality of the chocolate determines the difference between an average and great tasting cookie. Use the chocolate that tastes best to you.

1. Preheat oven to **375° F**. Line cookie sheets with parchment paper.

2. Sift flour, xanthan gum, baking soda and salt in bowl; stir. Set aside.

3. Beat melted butter, dark brown sugar, granulated sugar, vanilla and almond extracts in large mixer bowl on medium speed until just mixed, about 30 seconds. Beat in eggs, one at a time. Gradually beat in flour mixture. Stir in chocolate chips.

4. Measure dough in 2 tablespoon portions; drop 3 inches apart on prepared sheet.

5. Bake **12 to 13 minutes** or until edges are lightly browned. Cool 2 minutes on cookie sheet then transfer to wire rack to cool completely.

6. Store in airtight container up to 2 days or freeze up to 2 months.

Makes 2 dozen (3-inch) cookies

Variations:

 Reduce chocolate chips to ⅔ cup; add ⅓ cup white chocolate chunks and ⅓ cup toffee baking bits.

 Reduce chocolate chips to 1 cup; add ½ cup coarsely chopped walnuts or pecans.

Magical Macaroons

Attention coconut lovers! If you want an easy, versatile, beautiful-looking and chewy cookie to make, you've found it. It's magical, they will disappear right before your eyes... and no flour is required. (Photo page 12)

> 1 (14-oz.) can sweetened condensed milk (<u>not</u> evaporated milk)
> 1 teaspoon rum extract
> 2 teaspoons freshly grated lime zest
> 1 (14-oz.) package sweetened flaked coconut
> ½ cup finely chopped macadamia nuts
>
> 2 large egg whites
> ⅛ teaspoon salt

1. Preheat oven to **325° F.** Line cookie sheets with parchment paper.

2. Combine sweetened condensed milk, rum extract, lime zest, coconut and nuts in large bowl. Set aside.

3. Beat egg whites in small stainless steel bowl with handheld mixer until foamy, about 30 seconds. Add salt; beat on high speed until stiff peaks form, about 45 seconds. Using spatula, gently fold egg whites into coconut mixture.

4. Measure dough in 1½ tablespoon portions; drop 3 inches apart on prepared cookie sheets. Refrigerate remaining mixture until ready to bake.

5. Bake **16 to 18 minutes** or until coconut tips are golden brown. Watch closely because coconut burns. Cool 1 minute on cookie sheet then transfer to wire rack to cool completely.

6. Store in airtight container up to 3 days. Cookies soften as they sit.

Makes 2½ dozen (2-inch) cookies

Cookie Tips:

 Separate eggs (yolks from whites) while eggs are cold.

 Whipped egg whites produce greater volume when they are at <u>room temperature</u> and the bowl is clean and dry.

 Use leftover egg yolks in Lime Thumbprints (page 73) or Chocolate Crème-Filled Miniwiches (page 51).

Variation:

 Substitute freshly grated lemon zest, lemon extract and chopped pistachios for lime, rum extract, and macadamia nuts.

Oatmeal-Raisin Cookies

These time-tested favorites are chockfull of gluten-free oats and raisins. Why not have one or two for breakfast? If gluten-free oats are not in your diet, replace with quinoa flakes or soy flakes.

¾ cup The GF Cookie Lady's Flour (page 4)   ¼ teaspoon xanthan gum   ½ teaspoon baking soda   ¼ teaspoon salt   ¼ teaspoon freshly grated nutmeg   ¼ teaspoon ground cinnamon
½ cup (1 stick) unsalted butter, melted   ½ cup firmly packed light brown sugar   ¼ cup granulated sugar   ½ teaspoon pure vanilla extract
1 large egg
1½ cups gluten-free oats (Resources page 163)   ½ cup plump raisins*

1. Preheat oven to **350° F**. Line cookie sheets with parchment paper.
2. Sift flour, xanthan gum, baking soda, salt, nutmeg and cinnamon in bowl; stir. Set aside.
3. Combine melted butter, brown sugar, granulated sugar and vanilla in large bowl. Stir in egg. Gradually stir in flour mixture. Stir in oats and raisins.
4. Measure dough in 2 tablespoon portions; drop 4 inches apart on prepared sheet. Cookies spread. Keep dough refrigerated until ready to bake.
5. Bake **13 to 15 minutes** or until centers are soft and edges are lightly browned. Cool 5 minutes on cookie sheet then transfer to wire rack to cool completely. Cookies set up as they cool.
6. Store in airtight container up to 2 days or freeze up to 2 months.

Makes 15 (3½ -inch) cookies

Cookie Tip:

 *To plump raisins: cover raisins with hot liquid (water, juice, liqueurs) 3-7 minutes depending on their dryness. Drain and pat dry with paper towels.

Variations:

 If gluten-free oats are not in your diet, substitute with quinoa flakes or soy flakes. Find in health related grocery stores.

 Reduce raisin quantity by ¼ cup and add ¼ cup chopped walnuts.

Peanut Butter Cookies

These oh-so-easy, flourless cookies are very versatile and scored as winners by peanut butter lovers. Enjoy them plain, with a variety of add-ins or make cookie ice cream sandwiches. (Photo page 12)

1 cup granulated sugar
1 cup peanut butter
1 teaspoon baking soda
1 teaspoon pure vanilla extract
1 large egg

1. Preheat oven to **350° F.** Line cookie sheets with parchment paper.

2. Beat granulated sugar, peanut butter, baking soda and vanilla in large mixer bowl on medium speed until just mixed, about 30 seconds. Beat in egg.

3. Measure dough in 1½ tablespoon portions; drop 3 inches apart on prepared cookie sheet. With hand, flatten dough to ½-inch thickness.

4. Bake **11 to 13 minutes** or until tops are slightly cracked. Cool 4 minutes on cookie sheet then transfer to wire rack to cool completely. Garnish with granulated sugar, if desired.

5. Store in airtight container up to 3 days or freeze up to 2 months.

Makes almost 1½ dozen (3-inch) cookies

Cookie Tip:

 These cookies make great ice cream cookie sandwiches. Use your favorite ice cream flavor.

Variations:

Fold in ⅓ cup of toffee bits, raisins or M&Ms® for extra flavor, chew and crunch.

Bake cookies 9-10 minutes; remove from oven, place a chocolate kiss on top of each cookie and continue baking as directed.

PB & Oatmeal-Raisin Chipsters

What happens when you combine three favorite cookies into one? You'll get a champion-tasting, chewy cookie voted into the cookie hall of fame by the tasters. See if you agree.

½ cup The GF Cookie Lady's Flour (page 4)
¼ teaspoon xanthan gum
½ teaspoon baking soda
¼ teaspoon salt
½ teaspoon ground cinnamon
¼ teaspoon freshly grated nutmeg

½ cup (1 stick) unsalted butter
½ cup firmly packed dark brown sugar
½ cup granulated sugar
1 teaspoon pure vanilla extract

1 large egg
½ cup creamy peanut butter

1½ cups gluten-free oats*
½ cup raisins
½ cup semisweet chocolate chips

Cookie Tips:

 *Find supplier for gluten-free oats in Resources (page 163).

 Toast gluten-free oats for extra crunch. Spread oats in ungreased pan; bake in preheated 350° F oven 15 to 20 minutes, or until light golden brown.

Variation:

 If gluten-free oats are not in your diet, replace with quinoa flakes, a highly nutritious grain. Look for it at health related food markets.

1. Preheat oven to **350° F**. Line cookie sheets with parchment paper.

2. Sift flour, xanthan gum, baking soda, salt, cinnamon and nutmeg in large bowl; add oats, raisins and chocolate chips; stir. Set aside.

3. Beat butter, dark brown sugar, granulated sugar, and vanilla in large mixer bowl on medium speed until just mixed, about 30 seconds. Beat in egg and peanut butter. Gradually beat in flour mixture.

4. Measure dough in 1½ tablespoon portions; roll into balls and drop 3 inches apart on prepared sheet. With hand, slightly flatten each to ½-inch thickness.

5. Bake **13 to 15 minutes** or until golden brown but centers are slightly soft. Cool 4 minutes on cookie sheet then transfer to wire rack to cool completely. Cookies firm up as they sit.

6. Store in airtight container up to 2 days or freeze up to 2 months.

Makes 2 dozen (3-inch) cookies

Snickerdoodles

This versatile cookie was a celebrity among the taste testers and voted as one of the best! (Photo page 12)

1½ cups The GF Cookie Lady's Flour (page 4)   1¼ teaspoons xanthan gum   1 teaspoon cream of tartar   ½ teaspoon baking soda   ¼ teaspoon salt   ¼ teaspoon ground cinnamon
½ cup (1 stick) unsalted butter   1 cup granulated sugar   ½ teaspoon pure vanilla extract
1 large egg
1 tablespoon granulated sugar   1 teaspoon ground cinnamon   ⅛ teaspoon vanilla powder (optional)

Cookie Tip:

 Vanilla powder heightens the flavor of vanilla in any baked goods (Resources page 162).

1. Preheat oven to **350° F.** Line cookie sheets with parchment paper.

2. Sift flour, xanthan gum, cream of tartar, baking soda, salt and cinnamon in bowl; stir. Set aside.

3. Beat butter, granulated sugar and vanilla in large mixer bowl on medium speed until creamy, about 4 minutes. Beat in egg. Gradually beat in flour mixture.

4. Combine 1 tablespoon granulated sugar, 1 teaspoon ground cinnamon and ⅛ teaspoon vanilla powder in small bowl.

5. Measure dough in 1½ tablespoon portions; shape into balls and roll in cinnamon sugar mixture. Place balls 3 inches apart on prepared cookie sheet. With hand, flatten dough to ½-inch thickness.

6. Bake **12 to 13 minutes** or until edges are lightly browned. Cool 4 minutes on cookie sheet then transfer to wire rack to cool completely. Sprinkle remaining cinnamon sugar over cookies.

7. Store in airtight container up to 2 days or freeze up to 2 months.

Makes 1½ dozen (3-inch) cookies

Variation:

 For distinctive flavor, replace granulated sugar with vanilla-scented sugar (page 131).

Spicy Molasses Cookies

If you like the flavor of gingersnap cookies, you'll love these. Sweet, delicate spices and mild molasses make this soft and chewy cookie one of my personal favorites. (Photo page 12)

2¼ cups The GF Cookie Lady's Flour (page 4)
1½ teaspoons xanthan gum
2 teaspoons baking soda
¼ teaspoon salt
½ teaspoon ground cloves
1 teaspoon ground cinnamon
1 teaspoon ground ginger

¾ cup solid vegetable shortening
1 cup firmly packed light brown sugar

1 large egg
¼ cup mild unsulphured molasses

⅔ cup raisins (optional)

Cookie Tips:

- Unsulphured molasses means no additives are added. Find in baking aisle.
- Before measuring molasses, spray measuring cup with vegetable cooking spray to prevent molasses from sticking.

Variation:

- For extra flavor and crunch, roll dough balls in maple sugar (page 130) and finely crushed walnuts before baking.

1. Preheat oven to **375° F.** Line cookie sheets with parchment paper.

2. Sift flour, xanthan gum, baking soda, salt, cloves, cinnamon and ginger in bowl; stir. Set aside.

3. Beat shortening and brown sugar in large mixer bowl on medium speed until creamy, about 4 minutes. Beat in egg and molasses. Gradually beat in flour mixture. Stir in raisins, if desired.

4. Measure dough in 2 tablespoon portions. Shape into balls and roll in granulated sugar; place 3 inches apart on prepared cookie sheet. If necessary, refrigerate dough 30 minutes or until firm enough to roll into balls.

5. Bake **9 to 11 minutes** or until centers are set and tops have cracked. Cool 3 minutes on cookie sheet then transfer to wire rack to cool completely. Garnish with granulated sugar while cookies are still warm, if desired.

6. Store in airtight container up to 2 days or freeze up to 2 months.

Makes 2 dozen (3-inch) cookies

Spritz Cookies

Spritz cookies, a classic holiday treat, are baked to be shared. Decorative sugars give cookies a festive presentation. Happy Holidays!

2½ cups The GF Cookie Lady's Flour (page 4)
1½ teaspoons xanthan gum
½ teaspoon baking powder
¼ teaspoon salt

1 cup unsalted butter
1 cup vanilla-scented sugar (page 131) or granulated sugar
1 teaspoon pure almond extract
1 teaspoon pure vanilla extract

1 large egg
2 tablespoons heavy cream

1. Preheat oven to **400° F.** Place cookie sheets in freezer.
2. Sift flour, xanthan gum, baking powder and salt in bowl; stir. Set aside.
3. Beat butter, vanilla-scented sugar, almond and vanilla extracts in large mixer bowl on medium speed until creamy, about 4 minutes. Beat in egg and heavy cream. Gradually beat in flour mixture.
4. Fill cookie press with dough; press dough on **cold** sheet*, spacing 2 inches apart.
5. Bake **8 to 9 minutes** or until edges are very lightly browned. Cool 1 minute on cookie sheet then transfer to wire rack to cool completely. Garnish with vanilla-scented sugar, if desired.
6. Store in airtight container up to 2 days or freeze up to 2 months.

Makes over 4 dozen (2½- inch) cookies

Cookie Tips:

- Use a quality cookie press for easier baking.
- *For best results: Use a <u>cold</u> cookie sheet every time. Do not grease sheet or line with parchment paper.

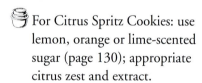

Variations:

- For Citrus Spritz Cookies: use lemon, orange or lime-scented sugar (page 130); appropriate citrus zest and extract.
- Sprinkle sugar over cookies before baking.

Sugar Cookies

Frosted or unfrosted, tasters said, "Simply the best".

2 cups The GF Cookie Lady's Flour (page 4)
1 teaspoon xanthan gum
½ teaspoon salt
½ teaspoon vanilla powder (Resources page 162)
¼ cup unsalted butter
¼ cup canola oil
⅔ cup granulated sugar
2 teaspoons pure vanilla extract
1 teaspoon pure almond extract
2 large egg yolks
1 tablespoon water
½ recipe Vanilla Cream Cheese Frosting (page 142)

1. Preheat oven to **350° F.** Line cookie sheets with parchment paper.
2. Sift flour, xanthan gum, salt and vanilla powder in bowl; stir. Set aside.
3. Beat butter, oil, granulated sugar, vanilla and almond extracts in large mixer bowl on medium speed until creamy, about 3 minutes. Beat in egg yolks and water. Gradually beat in flour mixture.
4. Measure dough in 1½ tablespoon portions; shape into balls and roll in sugar. Drop 3 inches apart on prepared sheet and flatten to ¼-inch thickness.
5. Bake **14 to 15 minutes** or until and edges are lightly browned. Cool 3 minutes on cookie sheet then transfer to wire rack to cool completely. **Frost**, if desired.
6. Store in airtight container up to 2 days or freeze up to 2 months.

Makes 1½ dozen (2-inch) cookies

Cookie Tips:

 Use flat-bottom dry measuring cup (1 cup size), dipped in sugar, to flatten cookies. Dip cup into sugar frequently to prevent dough from sticking. For thicker chewier cookies, flatten dough to ½–inch thickness and reduce baking time by 1 minute.

 Use leftover egg whites in Magical Macaroons (page 16) or almond paste (page 126).

Variation:

 Roll each ball of cookie dough in scented sugar (pages 130-131).

Best-Ever Bars and Brownies

Bars and brownies are some of the easiest and quickest gluten-free baked goods to make. Streusel-topped, caramel-layered, candy bar-filled—whatever your pleasure, there's a mouthwatering bar or brownie for you.

Here you can master one crust and enjoy four different bars such as, Cherry-Almond Cheesecake, Lemon Squares, Pecan Pie or Pumpkin Pie bars. How simple is that? Or make ooey, gooey Rocky Road Waffle Bars. Delicious, bar none!

You'll also find six brownie recipes to curb any sweet craving—from chewy and thick, cake-like or wickedly rich. Coffee lovers choose Brownie Double-Deckers; chocoholics try Fudgy Walnut Brownies; and for those of you who like a little chocolate flavor, the Frosted Cocoa Brownies. I am sure you'll find one that is just right for you.

- Apricot-Almond Bars 27
- Brownie Double-Deckers 28
- Candy Bar Brownies 30
- Caramel-Toffee Brownies 31
- Cherry-Almond Cheesecake Bars 32
- CranNutty Bars 33
- Date-Pecan Bars 34
- Frosted Cocoa Brownies 35
- Fudgy Walnut Brownies 36
- Lemon Squares 37
- Peanut Butter Brownies 38
- Pecan Pie Bars 39
- Pumpkin Pie Squares 40
- Raspberry-Marshmallow Brownies 41
- Rocky Road Waffle Bars 42
- Tropical Parfait Bars 43
- Ultimate Peanut-Marshmallow Bars 44

Pictured clockwise from upper left: Caramel-Toffee Brownies (p. 31), Raspberry-Marshmallow Brownies (p. 41), Fudgy Walnut Brownies (p. 36), Pecan Pie Bars (p. 39), Lemon Squares (p. 37), and Ultimate Peanut-Marshmallow Bars (p. 44)

Bar and Brownie Know-How:

Always use the size of pan specified in the recipe to prevent under or overbaking. Substituting other pan sizes changes baking times and may create uneven baking results. Bar/brownie recipes in this cookbook call for an 8 x 8 x 2-inch baking pan, unless stated differently.

Non-stick aluminum foil, such as Reynolds® Wrap Release®, is the best foil to use when making bars/brownies. No cooking spray or cleanup is required. When cool, lift foil with bars out of pan; peel foil away from sides and cut into desired portions.

For brownie recipes, use 1 quart glass measuring cup, such as Pyrex, to microwave butter and chocolate. Add remaining ingredients into same container to reduce cleanup.

Do not overmix brownies. Overmixing causes them to rise too much. As they cool, they will fall, making a cracked surface and an outer ridge. Prevent overmixing by using a wooden spoon or spatula rather than a free standing or handheld mixer.

Use a small (3½ -inch) offset spatula to smooth the surface of dough in the pan or apply frosting. It makes the job easier because the metal blade is lower than the handle. Find an offset spatula where kitchen gadgets are sold.

Use bottom of a flat measuring cup to press unbaked mixture firmly into the pan. To prevent dough from sticking to bottom of cup, keep surface clean; if needed, spray surface with non-stick cooking spray.

Bake brownies until just set. The meaning of "just set" is different depending on the type of brownie you're baking: For cake-like brownies, stick a toothpick in the center; it should come out almost clean. For a dense brownie, the toothpick should have some moist crumbs sticking to it. Brownies overbaked for even a few minutes will be much drier. Brownies will begin to retract around the edges of the pan; the top may have a faint puff to it; or small, hairline cracks may form.

To ensure the topping will adhere to the crust, it should always be placed on a warm baked crust.

Apply glazes while bars are slightly warm. A warm surface allows the glaze to spread more evenly, gives it a better sheen and helps it adhere.

To create sharp, clean and even edges, allow bars/brownies to cool completely before cutting them. Once cooled, put pan in the freezer for 15 minutes before cutting. Semi-frozen bars/brownies are easier to cut.

Use a ruler and toothpicks as a cutting guide. Strategically place toothpicks at each end; lay ruler across pan and cut into even portions. A bench scraper (found in kitchen specialty shops) is a useful cutting tool. It can be inserted down into the bar and lifted straight up, making clean even edges. Wipe tool clean after every cut.

Cut bars/brownies into other shapes for a different presentation. To make triangles, cut bars into rectangles and cut each diagonally into triangles. To make diamonds, first cut parallel lines 1 or 1½ inches apart down the length of the pan. Then cut diagonal lines the same distance apart across the pan, forming diamond shapes.

For Best Results:

- Read entire recipe to ensure necessary ingredients and equipment are on hand or if any advance procedure needs to be done.
- Have **all** ingredients at room temperature. Use quality ingredients.
- Preheat the oven at least 15 minutes. Keep ovenproof thermometer inside oven to ensure accurate temperature.
- Measure accurately and mix according to directions. Scrape bowl often to ensure homogenous dough.
- Check bars at the minimum baking time; continue baking, if necessary, in one-minute intervals. Every oven bakes a little differently.

Apricot-Almond Bars

If you like the combo of apricots and almonds—you've hit the jackpot. Try these extraordinary shortbread bars. If apricots are not a favorite, try raspberry for an equally dynamite flavor.

2 cups The GF Cookie Lady's Flour (page 4)
1 teaspoon xanthan gum
¼ teaspoon salt
¼ teaspoon ground cinnamon
¼ teaspoon freshly grated nutmeg

1 cup (2 sticks) unsalted butter
¾ cup granulated sugar
1 teaspoon pure almond extract

¼ cup packed almond paste (not marzipan) crumbled into small pieces

1 cup apricot jam
2 tablespoons orange juice
½ teaspoon pure vanilla extract

1 (2.25-oz.) package sliced almonds (equals ½ cup)

Cookie Tips:

 Notice there is no egg in this recipe.

 Not all almond pastes are gluten-free. Read labels or make your own (page 126).

1. Preheat oven to **325°F**. Line bottom and sides of 11 x 7-inch glass baking pan with non-stick aluminum foil; leave 1-inch overhang.

2. Sift flour, xanthan gum, salt, cinnamon and nutmeg in bowl; stir. Set aside.

3. Beat butter, granulated sugar and almond extract in large mixer bowl on medium speed until creamy, about 3 minutes. Beat in almond paste. Gradually beat in flour mixture.

4. Press half of the dough (1¼ cups) evenly in prepared pan. Combine apricot jam, orange juice and vanilla in small bowl. Spread apricot mixture over dough. Randomly drop the remaining dough (1¼ cups) in small increments on top of jam. Lightly press sliced almonds on dough.

5. Bake **58 to 60 minutes** or until toothpick inserted in center comes out clean and edges just start to pull away from sides. Cool in pan on wire rack. Remove from pan; cut into bars.

6. Store in airtight container up to 2 days or freeze up to 2 months.

Makes 14 bars

Variation:

To make Raspberry-Almond Bars, omit apricot preserves and orange juice and substitute with <u>seedless</u> raspberry preserves and apple juice.

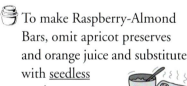

Brownie Double-Deckers

Fudge-like brownie on the bottom and chocolate chip cookie dough on top is what you'll find when you make these unusual, but wickedly delicious dessert. Double your pleasure with these double decker brownies!

Brownie Layer

⅓ cup The GF Cookie Lady's Flour (page 4)   ¼ teaspoon xanthan gum   ⅛ teaspoon salt   2 teaspoons <u>instant</u> coffee powder
¾ cup granulated sugar   6 tablespoons butter, melted   ⅓ cup unsweetened cocoa powder
1 large egg

Cookie Tip:

Unsweetened cocoa powder comes in two types: natural and Dutch-processed. Dutch-processed cocoa has a smoother more mellow flavor. Either can be use in this recipe.

Chocolate Chip Cookie Layer

¾ cup The GF Cookie Lady's Flour (page 4)   ½ teaspoon xanthan gum   ¼ teaspoon baking soda   ⅛ teaspoon salt
6 tablespoons butter, melted   ½ cup firmly packed light brown sugar   ½ teaspoon pure vanilla extract   ½ teaspoon pure almond extract
1 large egg
½ cup semisweet chocolate chips   1 (1.4-oz.) Heath® candy bar, coarsely chopped (equals ¼ cup)

Variation:

 For a distinctive flavor, substitute vanilla-scented sugar (page 131) for granulated sugar.

Directions continued on page 29.

1. Preheat oven to **325 ° F**. Line bottom and sides of an 8 x 8 x 2-inch pan with non-stick aluminum foil; leave 1-inch overhang.

2. **Brownie Layer**: Sift flour, xanthan gum, salt and instant coffee powder in bowl; stir. Set aside. Combine granulated sugar, melted butter and cocoa powder in large bowl. Stir in egg. Gradually stir in flour mixture. Spread dough evenly in prepared pan. Set aside.

3. **Chocolate Chip Layer**: Sift flour, xanthan gum, baking soda and salt in bowl; add chocolate chips and candy; stir. Set aside. Combine melted butter, brown sugar, vanilla and almond extracts in large bowl. Stir in egg. Gradually stir in flour mixture. Spread dough evenly over Brownie Layer.

4. Bake **38 to 40 minutes** or until toothpick inserted in center comes out almost clean and edges just start to pull away from sides.

5. Cool in pan on wire rack. Freeze 15 minutes; remove from pan and cut into portions.

6. Refrigerate brownies in airtight container up to 3 days or freeze up to 2 months.

Makes 16 brownies

Candy Bar Brownies

A large candy bar is baked into these chewy brownies making them popular with everyone.

¾ cup The GF Cookie Lady's Flour (page 4)
½ teaspoon xanthan gum
¼ cup unsweetened cocoa powder
¼ teaspoon baking soda
¼ teaspoon salt

6 tablespoons unsalted butter, melted
1 cup granulated sugar
½ teaspoon pure almond extract
1 teaspoon pure vanilla extract

2 large eggs

1 (5-oz.) Hershey's® Symphony candy bar, broken into sections

1. Preheat oven to **350° F**. Line bottom and sides of 8 x 8 x 2-inch pan with non-stick aluminum foil; leave 1-inch overhang.

2. Sift flour, xanthan gum, cocoa powder, baking soda and salt in bowl; stir. Set aside.

3. Combine melted butter, granulated sugar, almond and vanilla extracts in large bowl. Stir in eggs, one at a time. Gradually stir in flour mixture.

4. Spread half of dough (1 cup) evenly in prepared pan. Place candy pieces on dough. Using offset spatula, spread remaining dough (almost 1 cup) over candy.

5. Bake **30 to 32 minutes** or until toothpick inserted in center comes out almost clean and edges just start to pull away from sides. Cool in pan on wire rack. Remove from pan and cut into portions.

6. Store in airtight container up to 2 days or freeze up to 2 months.

Makes 16 brownies

Cookie Tip:

Instant cocoa mix which is filled with sugar and other ingredients is <u>not</u> suitable for baking. Use unsweetened cocoa powder for the best results. Well known brands are Hershey's and Ghirardelli.

Variation:

Replace Symphony candy bar with two (2.07-oz) Snickers®, cut into pieces. Stir candy pieces into dough. Gently press two (1.55-oz) milk chocolate candy bars, broken into pieces, on top of dough. Bake as directed.

Caramel-Toffee Brownies

If you like creamy caramel and chocolate, this fudgy brownie will send your taste buds soaring. (Photo page 24)

⅔ cup The GF Cookie Lady's Flour (page 4)   ½ teaspoon xanthan gum   ½ teaspoon baking powder   ¼ teaspoon salt
3 (1-oz.) squares unsweetened chocolate, coarsely chopped   6 tablespoons unsalted butter, cut into pieces
1 cup granulated sugar   1½ teaspoons pure vanilla extract   2 large eggs
1 recipe Caramel Crème Filling (page 137)
1 recipe Double Chip Glaze (page 145)
2 (2.07-oz.) Heath® candy bars, coarsely chopped

1. Preheat oven to **325° F.** Line bottom and sides of an 8 x 8 x 2-inch pan with non-stick aluminum foil; leave 1-inch overhang.

2. Sift flour, xanthan gum, baking powder and salt in bowl; stir. Set aside.

3. Put chocolate and butter in large microwave-safe bowl. Microwave, uncovered, on High (100 percent power) in 30 second intervals until melted. Stir after each interval. Cool 5 minutes. Stir granulated sugar, vanilla and eggs into chocolate mixture. Stir in flour mixture. Spread dough evenly in prepared pan.

4. Bake **32 to 34 minutes** or until toothpick inserted in center comes out almost clean and edges just start to pull away from sides.

5. Make **Caramel Crème Filling** as brownies bake. Pour <u>hot</u> filling immediately over <u>hot</u> brownies. Cool in pan on wire rack. Freeze 15 minutes before frosting to set caramel layer.

6. **Frost** and garnish with candy pieces. Freeze another 15 minutes; remove from pan and cut into portions.

7. Refrigerate brownies in airtight container up to 3 days or freeze, unfrosted, up to 2 months.

Makes 16 brownies

Cookie Tips:

 The darker the chocolate is the higher its antioxidant content. Enjoy!

 Two (2.07-oz) candy bars is equivalent to ½ cup coarsely chopped; or use ½ cup English toffee baking bits.

Variations:

 To make Mocha-Toffee Brownies, replace Caramel Crème Filling with Mocha Filling (page 138). Note: spread mocha filling over <u>cooled</u> brownies and continue with recipe.

Cherry-Almond Cheesecake Bars

Splurge on these rich and fruity cheesecake bars when you crave for something heavenly. Topped with a scrumptious streusel, you'll be hooked forever.

Crust:	1 cup The GF Cookie Lady's Flour (page 4) 1 teaspoon xanthan gum ¼ cup firmly packed light brown sugar 5 tablespoons cold butter, cut into small pieces
Filling:	1 (8-oz.) package cream cheese ¼ cup granulated sugar 1 large egg ½ teaspoon pure vanilla extract
Fruit Layer:	1 (21-oz.) can cherry pie filling 1 teaspoon pure almond extract 2-3 tablespoons almond slices
Streusel Topping:	¼ cup The GF Cookie Lady's Flour (page 4) ⅛ teaspoon xanthan gum ¼ cup firmly packed light brown sugar 2 tablespoons gluten-free oats* 2 tablespoons butter, cut into chunks

Cookie Tips:

 *Find suppliers of gluten-free oats in Resources (page 163).

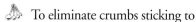 To eliminate crumbs sticking to your hands, lay a piece of waxed paper over crumb mixture as you press it into pan.

1. Preheat oven to **350° F.** Line bottom and sides of 8 x 8 x 2-inch baking pan with non-stick aluminum foil; leave 1-inch overhang.

2. **Crust:** Beat flour, xanthan gum, brown sugar and butter in large mixer bowl on medium speed until crumbly, about 1½ minutes. Press mixture firmly in prepared pan. Bake **16 minutes.** (Make remaining layers as crust bakes.)

3. **Filling:** Beat cream cheese in large mixer bowl on medium speed until creamy, about 1½ minutes. Beat in granulated sugar, egg and vanilla until well mixed, about 2 minutes. Pour over <u>hot</u> crust.

4. **Fruit Layer:** Combine cherry pie filling, almond extract and almond slices. Spread evenly over cream cheese layer.

5. **Streusel Topping:** Combine flour, xanthan gum, brown sugar, oats and butter until crumbly. Drop oat mixture over fruit layer; pat down with hand. Return pan to oven. Bake another **29-32 minutes** or until toothpick inserted in center comes out clean and edges just start to pull away from sides. Cool in pan on wire rack. Remove from pan and cut into bars.

6. Refrigerate bars in airtight container up to 3 days.

Makes 16 bars

Variations:

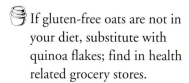 If gluten-free oats are not in your diet, substitute with quinoa flakes; find in health related grocery stores.

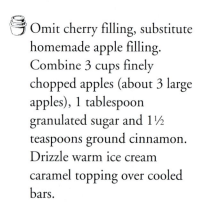 Omit cherry filling, substitute homemade apple filling. Combine 3 cups finely chopped apples (about 3 large apples), 1 tablespoon granulated sugar and 1½ teaspoons ground cinnamon. Drizzle warm ice cream caramel topping over cooled bars.

CranNutty Bars

Tart cranberries, crunchy pecans, sweet white chocolate and a creamy frosting make these bars a cut above the rest.

1 cup plus 2 tablespoons The GF Cookie Lady's Flour (page 4) 1 teaspoon xanthan gum ¾ teaspoon baking powder ½ teaspoon salt ½ teaspoon ground cinnamon
½ cup (1 stick) unsalted butter ¾ cup firmly packed light brown sugar 1 teaspoon pure vanilla extract ½ teaspoon pure orange oil*
1 large egg
¾ cup white chocolate chips ½ cup dried cranberries ¾ cup coarsely chopped pecans
1 recipe Cranberry Cream Cheese Frosting (page 142)

Cookie Tip:

 *Pure orange oil is found in kitchen specialty stores (Resources page 164). If unavailable, use 1 teaspoon of orange extract or 2 teaspoons freshly grated orange zest.

Variation:

 Garnish with dried cranberries and pecans.

1. Preheat oven to **350° F**. Line bottom and sides of 8 x 8 x 2-inch baking pan with non-stick aluminum foil, leave 1-inch overhang.

2. Sift flour, xanthan gum, baking powder, salt and cinnamon in bowl, stir. Set aside.

3. Beat butter, brown sugar, vanilla and orange oil in large mixer bowl on medium speed until well mixed, about 2 minutes. Beat in egg. Gradually beat in flour mixture. Beat in white chocolate chips, cranberries and pecans. Spread dough evenly in prepared pan.

4. Bake **30 to 32 minutes** or until toothpick inserted in center comes out clean and edges just start to pull away from sides. Cool in pan on wire rack.

5. **Frost**; remove from pan and cut into bars.

6. Refrigerate bars in airtight container up to 3 days or freeze, unfrosted, up to 2 months.

Makes 16 bars

Date-Pecan Bars

*Dates and pecans team up to hit your sweet tooth in these chewy, golden brown bars.
They are easy to make and do not require a mixer.*

¾ cup The GF Cookie Lady's Flour (page 4) ½ teaspoon xanthan gum 1 teaspoon baking powder ⅛ teaspoon salt ¼ teaspoon ground cinnamon
¼ cup (½ stick) unsalted butter, melted and slightly cooled 1 cup firmly packed light brown sugar ½ teaspoon rum extract ½ teaspoon caramel flavoring*
1 large egg
¼ cup coarsely chopped pecans ¼ cup dates, cut into small pieces

1. Preheat oven to **350° F**. Line bottom and sides of 8 x 8 x 2-inch baking pan with non-stick aluminum foil; leave 1-inch overhang.

2. Sift flour, xanthan gum, baking powder, salt and cinnamon in bowl; add pecans and dates; stir. Set aside.

3. Combine melted butter, brown sugar, rum extract and caramel flavoring in large bowl. Stir in egg. Gradually stir in flour mixture.

4. Bake **20 to 22 minutes** or until toothpick inserted in center comes out clean and edges just start to pull away from sides. Cool in pan on wire rack. Remove from pan and cut into bars.

5. Store in airtight container up to 2 days or freeze up to 2 months.

Makes 16 bars

Cookie Tips:

 *Caramel flavoring is the secret ingredient in this recipe (Resources page 164).

 Kitchen scissors cut dates easier than a knife.

Variation:

 For a pretty presentation, sprinkle confectioners' sugar over bars.

Frosted Cocoa Brownies

Here is a mild chocolate, cake-like brownie made with unsweetened cocoa powder and topped with a decadent frosting. Serve with homemade vanilla ice cream, these brownies will be requested often.

1 cup The GF Cookie Lady's Flour (page 4)
1 cup granulated sugar
¼ teaspoon xanthan gum
½ teaspoon baking soda
¼ teaspoon salt
¼ teaspoon ground cinnamon
½ cup (1 stick) unsalted butter, cut into pieces
⅓ cup hot water
2 tablespoons unsweetened cocoa powder
1 large egg
¼ cup buttermilk
1 teaspoon pure vanilla extract
1 recipe Fudge Frosting (page 144)

Cookie Tip:

 For a smooth silky finish, frost brownies while warm.

1. Preheat oven to **350° F.** Line bottom and sides of 8 x 8 x 2-inch baking pan with non-stick aluminum foil; leave 1 inch overhang.

2. Sift flour, granulated sugar, xanthan gum, baking soda, salt and cinnamon in large bowl; stir. Set aside.

3. Combine butter, water and cocoa powder in small saucepan; bring mixture to rapid boil over medium high heat, stirring frequently. Pour boiling mixture over flour mixture; stir. Stir in egg, buttermilk and vanilla. Spread dough evenly in prepared pan.

4. Bake **28 to 32 minutes** or until toothpick inserted in center comes out clean and edges just start to pull away from sides. Let stand 5 minutes then **Frost**.

5. Cool in pan on wire rack. Freeze 15 minutes; remove from pan and cut into portions.

6. Refrigerate brownies in airtight container up to 3 days or freeze, unfrosted, up to 2 months.

Variation:

Add ¼ cup chopped pecans and ¼ cup sweetened flake coconut to frosting for added crunch and flavor.

Makes 16 brownies

Fudgy Walnut Brownies

Loads of semisweet chocolate chips and walnuts make for a rich scrumptious brownie that chocolate lovers will ask for over and over again. (Photo page 24)

½ cup The GF Cookie Lady's Flour (page 4)   ⅛ teaspoon xanthan gum   ¼ teaspoon baking powder   ¼ teaspoon salt   2 teaspoons vanilla-flavored <u>instant</u> coffee powder
6 tablespoons unsalted butter, cut into pieces   2 cups semisweet chocolate chips
3 large eggs   1 teaspoon pure vanilla extract   1 cup granulated sugar
1 cup semisweet chocolate chips   1 cup coarsely chopped walnuts

Cookie Tip:

Chocolate flavor is intensified with coffee. For a stronger coffee flavor, use your favorite espresso powder.

1. Preheat oven to **350° F**. Line bottom and sides of 8 x 8 x 2-inch baking pan with non-stick aluminum foil; leave 1 inch overhang.

2. Sift flour, xanthan gum, baking powder, salt and instant coffee powder in bowl; add 1 cup chocolate chips and nuts; stir. Set aside.

3. Put butter and 2 cups chocolate chips in microwave-safe bowl. Microwave, uncovered, on High (100 percent power) in 30 second intervals until melted. Stir after each interval. Cool 5 minutes. Beat eggs, vanilla and granulated sugar in large mixer bowl on medium speed until creamy, about 3 minutes. Stir in chocolate mixture. Stir in flour mixture. Spread dough evenly in prepared pan.

4. Bake **40 to 42 minutes** or until toothpick inserted in center comes out almost clean and edges just start to pull away from sides. Brownies have a few cracks on top. Cool in pan on wire rack at least 2 hours. Remove from pan and cut into portions.

5. Store in airtight container up to 2 days or freeze up to 2 months.

Makes 16 brownies

Variation:

 Substitute vanilla-scented sugar for granulated sugar (page 131) and flavored nuts (page 127) for plain walnuts for an extra flavor bonus.

Lemon Squares

Easy-to-make and so delightfully delicious, lemon connoisseurs will love these bars. Not a lemon lover? Try lime or orange for an equally tasty treat. (Photo page 24)

Crust:	1 cup Cookie Lady's GF Flour (page 4) 1 teaspoon xanthan gum ¼ teaspoon freshly grated lemon zest ⅛ teaspoon ground cardamom ¼ cup citrus-scented sugar–lemon (page 130) 5 tablespoons cold unsalted butter, cut into small chunks
Filling:	2 tablespoons The GF Cookie Lady's Flour 1 cup citrus-scented sugar–lemon ½ teaspoon baking powder ⅛ teaspoon salt 2 large eggs 3 tablespoons freshly squeezed lemon juice (1 large lemon) 1 teaspoon freshly grated lemon zest ½ teaspoon pure lemon oil*

Cookie Tips:

 Granulated sugar may be used, but lemon-scented sugar adds a new flavor dimension.

 *Find pure lemon oil in kitchen specialty stores (Resources page 164). If you can't find lemon oil, use 1 teaspoon of lemon extract or double lemon zest.

1. Preheat oven to **350° F.** Line bottom and sides of 8 x 8 x 2-inch pan with non-stick aluminum foil; leave 1-inch overhang.

2. **Crust:** Beat flour, xanthan gum, lemon zest, cardamom, lemon-scented sugar and butter in large mixer bowl on medium speed until crumbly, about 1½ minutes. Press mixture in prepared pan. Bake **15 to 16 minutes.** (Make filling as crust bakes.)

3. **Filling:** Beat flour, lemon-scented sugar, baking powder, salt, eggs, lemon juice, lemon zest and lemon oil in large mixer bowl on medium speed until well mixed, about 1 minute. Pour filling immediately over <u>hot</u> crust and return to oven. Bake another **18 to 20 minutes** or until toothpick inserted in center comes out clean and edges just start to pull away from sides.

4. Cool in pan on wire rack. Remove from pan and cut into bars.

5. Refrigerate bars in airtight container up to 3 days.

Makes 16 bars

Variations:

 Sprinkle confectioners' sugar over cooled bars for an attractive presentation.

 Pour Lemon Glaze (page 146) over warm bars for a citrus extravagance.

Peanut Butter Brownies

Start with a chewy brownie, add creamy peanut butter filling and chunks of peanut butter cups, and you have a treat that will soon be addictive.

⅔ cup The GF Cookie Lady's Flour (page 4)
½ teaspoon xanthan gum
½ teaspoon baking powder
¼ teaspoon salt
3 (1-oz.) squares unsweetened chocolate, coarsely chopped
6 tablespoons unsalted butter, cut into pieces
1 cup granulated sugar
1½ teaspoons pure vanilla extract
2 large eggs
1 recipe Peanut Butter Filling (page 139)
1 recipe Peanut Butter Cream Cheese Frosting (page 142)
16 miniature peanut butter cups

Cookie Tip:

 A warm surface allows filling to spread more evenly and helps it adhere.

1. Preheat oven to **325 °F**. Line bottom and sides of 8 x 8 x 2-inch pan with non-stick aluminum foil; leave 1-inch overhang.

2. Sift flour, xanthan gum, baking powder and salt in bowl; stir. Set aside.

3. Put chocolate and butter in large microwave-safe bowl. Microwave, uncovered, on High (100 percent power) in 30 second intervals until melted. Stir after each interval. Cool 5 minutes. Stir granulated sugar, vanilla and eggs into chocolate mixture. Stir in flour mixture. Spread dough evenly in prepared pan.

4. Bake **32 to 34 minutes** or until toothpick inserted in center comes out almost clean and edges just start to pull away from sides. (Make **Peanut Butter Filling** while brownies bake.) Let brownies stand 4 minutes then spread filling on top. Cool completely.

5. **Frost**. Place miniature peanut butter cups (4 rows x 4 rows) on frosting. Freeze 15 minutes; remove from pan and cut into portions.

6. Refrigerate brownies in airtight container up to 3 days or freeze, unfrosted, up to 2 months.

Makes 16 brownies

Variations:

- Omit peanut butter cups and replace with ½ cup chopped peanuts sprinkled on top.

- For Mint Brownies, replace filling, frosting and garnish with Mint Filling (page 138) and Chocolate Glaze (page 145) and gluten-free peppermint candies. Spread mint filling over <u>cooled</u> brownies.

Pecan Pie Bars

Make these bars instead of going to the trouble of baking a pecan pie. Enjoy these easy-to-make, gooey bars any time of year, not just around the holidays. (Photo page 24)

Crust:	1 cup The GF Cookie Lady's Flour (page 4) 1 teaspoon xanthan gum ⅛ teaspoon freshly grated nutmeg ¼ cup granulated sugar 5 tablespoons cold unsalted butter, cut into small chunks
Filling:	¼ cup unsalted butter, melted ½ cup firmly packed light brown sugar ⅓ cup dark corn syrup 1 tablespoon pure vanilla extract ½ teaspoon salt 1 large egg 1½ cups coarsely chopped pecans

Cookie Tip:

 Pecans are an excellent source of protein, add fiber to your diet and contain iron, calcium, vitamins A, B and C, potassium and phosphorous. Go nuts!

1. Preheat oven to **350° F.** Line bottom and sides of 8 x 8 x 2-inch pan with non-stick aluminum foil; leave 1-inch overhang.

2. **Crust**: Beat flour, xanthan gum, nutmeg, granulated sugar and butter in large mixer bowl on medium speed until crumbly, about 1½ minutes. Press mixture firmly in prepared pan. Bake **15 minutes**. (Make filling as crust bakes.)

3. **Filling:** Combine melted butter, brown sugar, dark corn syrup, vanilla, salt, egg, and pecans in bowl. Pour filling immediately over <u>hot</u> crust and return to oven. Bake another **27 to 29 minutes** or until toothpick inserted in center comes out clean and edges just start to pull away from sides.

4. Cool in rack on wire rack. Remove from pan and cut into bars.

5. Refrigerate bars in airtight container up to 3 days or freeze up to 2 months.

Makes 16 bars

Variation:

 For scrumptious flavor, replace granulated sugar in recipe with maple-scented sugar (page 130) and use Maple Nuts (page 128).

Best-Ever Bars and Brownies

Pumpkin Pie Squares

*These bars are made with 100% pure pumpkin.
Don't wait until Thanksgiving to make these healthy little winners, enjoy them year round.*

Crust:	1 cup The GF Cookie Lady's Flour (page 4) 1 teaspoon xanthan gum ⅛ teaspoon ground cinnamon ¼ cup granulated sugar 5 tablespoons cold unsalted butter, cut into small chunks
Filling:	½ (15-oz.) can 100% pure pumpkin (equals 1 cup) ½ (12-oz.) can evaporated milk (equals ¾ cup) 1 large egg ⅓ cup granulated sugar ¼ teaspoon salt ⅛ teaspoon ground cloves ¼ teaspoon ground ginger ½ teaspoon freshly grated nutmeg 1½ teaspoons ground cinnamon
Topping:	⅓ cup finely chopped pecans

1. Preheat oven to **350° F.** Line bottom and sides of an 8 x 8 x 2-inch pan with non-stick aluminum foil; leave 1-inch overhang.

2. **Crust:** Beat flour, xanthan gum, cinnamon, granulated sugar and butter in large mixer bowl on medium speed until crumbly, about 1½ minutes. Press mixture firmly in prepared pan. Bake **15 minutes.** (Make filling as crust bakes.)

3. **Filling:** Combine pumpkin, evaporated milk, egg, granulated sugar, salt, cloves, ginger, nutmeg and cinnamon in bowl. Pour filling immediately over <u>hot</u> crust and return to oven. Bake **22 minutes.** Remove pan from oven; sprinkle pecans on top. Bake another **18 to 20 minutes** or until toothpick inserted in center comes out clean and edges just start to pull away from sides.

4. Cool in pan on wire rack. Remove from pan and cut into bars.

5. Refrigerate bars in airtight container up to 3 days or freeze up to 2 months.

Makes 16 bars

Cookie Tips:

- Pumpkin is excellent source of vitamin C, fiber and potassium.

- Make another pan of bars and use remaining pumpkin and evaporated milk. Enjoy one now and freeze one for later.

Variations:

- For an outstanding flavor, substitute maple-scented sugar (page 130) for granulated sugar in crust and filling.

- Replace topping with flavored nuts (pages 127-128) for extra pizzazz.

Raspberry-Marshmallow Brownies

Blast off with these dense, rich brownies layered with raspberry marshmallows. (Photo page 24)

⅔ cup The GF Cookie Lady's Flour (page 4)   ½ teaspoon xanthan   1 teaspoon baking powder   ⅛ teaspoon salt   ¼ teaspoon ground cinnamon
2 tablespoons solid vegetable shortening   1¼ cups firmly packed light brown sugar   1 teaspoon pure vanilla extract
2 (1-oz.) squares unsweetened chocolate, melted and cooled   2 large eggs
3 tablespoons <u>seedless</u> raspberry preserves   1½ cups miniature marshmallows

1. Preheat oven to **350° F**. Line bottom and sides of 8 x 8 x 2-inch baking pan with non-stick aluminum foil; leave 1-inch overhang.

2. Sift flour, xanthan gum, baking powder, salt and cinnamon in bowl; stir.

3. Combine shortening, brown sugar and vanilla in large bowl. Stir in melted chocolate and eggs. Stir in flour mixture. Spread dough evenly in prepared pan.

4. Bake **21 to 24 minutes** or until toothpick inserted in center comes out almost clean and top begins to crack.

5. Heat raspberry preserves in small microwave-safe bowl on High (100 percent power) 10 to 15 seconds. Remove from microwave; stir in marshmallows. Using offset spatula, gently spread marshmallow mixture over hot brownies. Return pan to oven **2 to 3 minutes** or just until marshmallows begin to puff.

6. Cool in pan on wire rack. Freeze 15 minutes; remove from pan and cut into portions.

7. Refrigerate bars in airtight container up to 3 days or freeze up to 2 months.

Makes 16 brownies

Cookie Tip:

 Solid vegetable shortening such as Crisco® may be purchased in two varieties: Traditional All Vegetable or Butter Flavor. Both have no trans fat and either variety may be used.

Variations:

 Add ¼ cup chopped pecans and ½ cup baking toffee bits to dry ingredients for added crunch and flavor.

 Drizzle Chocolate Glaze (page 145) over marshmallows for a classy presentation.

Rocky Road Waffle Bars

These bars are simply irresistible. Four gluten-free waffles form the crust followed by eight ooey gooey layers. Yum!

4 (4-inch) gluten-free waffles (page 148)
⅓ cup semisweet chocolate chips
⅓ cup butterscotch chips
⅓ cup peanut butter chips
⅓ cup sweetened flaked coconut
⅓ cup dry roasted peanuts
1 cup sweetened condensed milk (see Tip)
⅓ cup sweetened condensed milk
16 light-colored caramels, unwrapped
1 recipe for Double Chip Glaze (page 145)

Cookie Tips:

- Store-bought gluten-free waffles may be used; but homemade waffles (page 148) are the best and do make a big difference.

- One (14-oz.) can sweetened condensed milk is equal to 1⅓ cups. This recipe takes the whole can, 1 cup for the bars and ⅓ cup for caramel topping.

- Read labels for hidden gluten in butterscotch chips and dry roasted peanuts.

1. Preheat oven to **350° F.** Line bottom and sides of an 8 x 8 x 2-inch baking pan with non-stick aluminum foil; leave 1-inch overhang.

2. Place waffles (do not overlap) in prepared pan. Layer flavored chips, coconut and peanuts as listed. Pour 1 cup sweetened condensed milk over layers. Bake **20 to 22 minutes** or until edges just start to pull away from sides.

3. Combine remaining sweetened condensed milk (1/3 cup) and caramels in large microwave-safe bowl. Microwave, uncovered, on High (100 percent power) in 30 second intervals until melted. Stir after each interval. Pour caramel filling over hot bars.

4. Cool in pan on wire rack until caramel is set. Freeze 15 minutes before frosting.

5. **Frost.** Freeze another 15 minutes; remove from pan and cut into bars.

6. Refrigerate bars in airtight container up to 4 days.

Makes 16 bars

Tropical Parfait Bars

These moist cake-like bars topped with a luscious frosting are outrageously delicious. No added fat, just fruits and nuts are packed inside for a tropical delight.

1½ cups The GF Cookie Lady's Flour (page 4)   1 teaspoon xanthan gum   ½ teaspoon baking soda   1 teaspoon baking powder   ½ teaspoon salt   ½ teaspoon ground cinnamon
1 cup granulated sugar   1 teaspoon pure vanilla extract   1 large egg
½ cup mashed banana (7-inch banana)   1 (8-oz.) can crushed pineapple, <u>well drained</u>*   ½ cup coarsely chopped macadamia nuts   ¼ cup sweetened flaked coconut
½ recipe for Pineapple Cream Cheese Frosting (page 142)

Cookie Tips:

 *If pineapple isn't well drained, bars may be soggy. Drain; squeeze to remove liquid until 5 tablespoons of pineapple remain.

 These bars cut easier if placed in freezer 15-20 minutes before cutting. Wash knife after each cut for nice clean cuts.

1. Preheat oven to **350° F.** Line bottom and sides of an 8 x 8 x 2-inch baking pan with non-stick aluminum foil; leave 1-inch overhang.

2. Sift flour, xanthan gum, baking soda, baking powder, salt and cinnamon in bowl; stir. Set aside.

3. Combine granulated sugar, vanilla and egg in large bowl. Stir in flour mixture. Combine banana, well drained pineapple, nuts and coconut; stir into dough. Use lightly moistened fingers to press dough evenly in prepared pan.

4. Bake **35 to 40 minutes** or until toothpick inserted in center comes out clean and edges pull away from sides. Cool in pan on wire rack.

5. **Frost**. Freeze 15 minutes; remove from pan and cut into bars.

6. Refrigerate bars in airtight container up to 3 days or freeze, unfrosted, up to 2 months.

Makes 16 bars

Variation:

 Replace vanilla, cinnamon and macadamias with rum extract, walnuts and ground ginger for an equally delightful flavor.

Best-Ever Bars and Brownies

Ultimate Peanut-Marshmallow Bars

This gourmet-looking cookie made in a fluted tart pan wins on all counts- quick, easy to make and so delicious. It's the ultimate dessert showstopper and will surely impress family and friends. (Photo page 24 and 45)

¾ cup The GF Cookie Lady's Flour (page 4)
½ teaspoon xanthan gum
¼ teaspoon baking powder
¼ teaspoon baking soda
¼ teaspoon salt

¼ cup (½ stick) unsalted butter
⅓ cup firmly packed light brown sugar
½ teaspoon pure vanilla extract

1 large egg yolk

1½ cups miniature marshmallows

Peanut Butter Topping:
3 tablespoons light corn syrup
1 tablespoon unsalted butter
⅓ cup peanut butter chips
½ teaspoon pure vanilla extract
1 cup dry roasted salted peanuts

Chocolate Chip Topping:
3 tablespoons light corn syrup
1 tablespoon unsalted butter
⅓ cup semisweet chocolate chips
½ teaspoon vanilla extract
1 cup dry roasted salted peanuts

Cookie Tips:

- To save tart pan from knife marks, slide cookie off pan before cutting.

- Use a pizza wheel cutter to cut these thin-crusted bars.

Variation:

For beautiful presentation, make variegated wheel design with toppings. Drop chocolate topping by teaspoonful around outer edge, forming a 1-inch border. Then drop peanut butter topping to form the next border; continue alternating toppings until cookie is completely covered.

1. Preheat oven to **350° F.** Spray 10-inch tart pan (with removable bottom) with vegetable cooking spray.

2. Sift flour, xanthan gum, baking powder, baking soda and salt in bowl; stir. Set aside.

3. Beat butter, brown sugar and vanilla in large mixer bowl on medium speed until creamy, about 3 minutes. Beat in egg yolk. Gradually beat in flour mixture. With lightly moistened fingers, press dough evenly in bottom and 1/8-inch up sides of prepared pan.

(continued on page 45)

4. Bake **8 to 10 minutes** or until edges are lightly browned. Remove pan from oven; place marshmallows in single layer on crust. Return to oven until marshmallows begin to puff, about 2 minutes.

5. Make **Peanut Butter Topping** as crust bakes. Combine corn syrup, butter and peanut butter chips in microwave-safe bowl. Microwave, uncovered, on High (100 percent power) in 30 second intervals until melted. Stir after each interval. Remove from microwave; stir in vanilla and peanuts.

6. Make **Chocolate Chip Topping** as crust bakes: Combine corn syrup, butter and chocolate chips in another microwave-safe bowl. Microwave, uncovered, on High (100 percent power) in 30 second intervals until melted. Stir after each interval. Remove from microwave; stir in vanilla and peanuts.

7. Remove pan from oven; immediately drop peanut butter and chocolate toppings by tablespoonfuls over marshmallows. Use fingertips to carefully spread toppings.

8. Cool in pan on wire rack. Refrigerate 30 minutes; remove from pan and cut into bars.

9. Refrigerate bars in airtight container up to 3 days.

Makes 15 bars

Ultimate Peanut-Marshmallow Bars

46 Chocolate-Lover Cookies

Chocolate-Lover Cookies

Calling all chocolate fans: white and milk chocolate, bittersweet, semisweet and unsweetened chocolate await you. As chocolate lovers attest, you can never get too much chocolate. Chocolate aficionado testers loved Triple Chocolate Macadamia and White Chocolate-Macadamia. They said both belong in the Cookie Gourmet Hall of Fame.

- Cherry-Chocolate Chews 49
- Chocolate Chip Pralines 50
- Chocolate Crème-Filled Miniwiches 51
- Chocolate Macaroons 52
- Chocolate-Minty Marvels 53
- Chocolate Roloz 54
- Chocolate Surprise Balls 55
- Chocolate Waffle Cookies 56
- Double Chocolate Delights 57
- Triple Chocolate Bliss 58
- White Chocolate-Macadamia 59

Top: Double Chocolate Delights (p. 57)
Middle: Chocolate Roloz (p. 54)
Bottom: White Chocolate-Macadamia (p. 59), Triple Chocolate Bliss (p. 58)
Napkin: Chocolate Crème-Filled Miniwiches (p. 51)

Chocolate Know-How:

Not all chocolate or chocolate chips are created equal. It's the quality of the chocolate that determines the difference between a good and a great chocolate cookie. To assess a chocolate's quality, read the label and look for a high cocoa-solid content, the best chocolate contains 50 percent or more.

Well-known domestic brands include Baker's, Ghirardelli, Guittard and Scharffen Berger. Premium imported chocolate, such as Callebaut (from Belgium), El Rey (from Venezuela), Lindt (from Switzerland), and Valrhona (from France) are now widely available in supermarkets or specialty stores. Bake with the chocolate that tastes best to you. Price and personal preference will dictate which chocolate to use.

Unsweetened cocoa powder is made from ground roasted cocoa beans. It is pure with no added ingredients. Two types of cocoa powder used in baking are **natural** such as Hershey's and **Dutch-processed** such as Droste. Natural cocoa powder is acidic and has a strong full-bodied, more chocolate flavor. Dutch-processed cocoa has been treated with an alkaline solution to reduce the natural acidity. It is darker in color and has a milder more delicate flavor. Do not substitute an instant cocoa mix which is filled with sugar and other ingredients.

Unsweetened chocolate is made from pure chocolate liquor, about 45 to 47 percent, and must contain 53 to 55 percent cocoa butter. It has healthy antioxidant properties but has a bitter taste and relies on sweeteners in the recipe to make it palatable. Wrapped individually in 1-oz. squares, it is available in 8-oz. boxes. Do not substitute semisweet or bittersweet for unsweetened chocolate.

Bittersweet and semisweet have sugar, lecithin (a natural soybean product), and vanilla added. These products must contain at least 27 percent cocoa butter. Bittersweet must have at least 35 percent chocolate liquor; while semisweet has 15 to 35 percent chocolate liquor. Bittersweet and semisweet chocolate are interchangeable in recipes and may be found individually wrapped in 1-oz. squares or chips.

Milk chocolate is sweetened chocolate to which dry milk powder, sugar and vanilla have been added. It must contain at least 10 percent chocolate liquor and minimum of 12 percent milk solids.

White chocolate is not considered "real" chocolate because it contains no chocolate liquor. It is made of sugar, cocoa butter, milk solids, lecithin and vanilla. Quality white chocolate has a creamy color, contains high cocoa butter content and no vegetable shortening. Read the label and check the ingredients for the words "cocoa butter" listed as the <u>second ingredient</u>, if not listed, don't purchase. Imitation white chocolate is made with vegetable oil instead of cocoa butter and has a waxy, inferior flavor. It will not perform the same as a product with cocoa butter.

To store chocolate: Keep chocolate in a cool (ideal temperature between 65 and 70°) dark place away from heat, light and moisture. Well wrapped and stored properly, unsweetened, bittersweet and semisweet chocolate keep up to 18 months. A dusty white coating called "bloom" may appear on chocolate during storage. There is nothing wrong with the chocolate except its appearance.

Milk and white chocolate, due to their high milk contents, have a much shorter shelf life and can go rancid easily. Use milk chocolate within 6 months and white chocolate within 4 months of purchase.

For Best Results:

- Read entire recipe to ensure necessary ingredients and equipment are on hand or if any advance procedure needs to be done.

- Have **all** ingredients at room temperature. Use quality ingredients.

- Preheat the oven at least 15 minutes. Keep ovenproof thermometer inside oven to ensure accurate temperature.

- Measure accurately and mix according to directions. Scrape bowl often to ensure homogenous dough.

- Use spring-release cookie scoop for uniform size that bakes evenly and at same time.

- Bake one cookie sheet at a time on the middle rack of the oven. Use quality cookie sheets.

- Check cookies at the minimum baking time; continue baking, if necessary, in one-minute intervals. Every oven bakes a little differently. Bake one "test" cookie to gauge baking time in <u>your</u> oven. Better to underbake than overbake.

Cherry-Chocolate Chews

*Chocolate, tart cherries and hazelnuts team up to provide the perfect sweet treat.
Tasters said these cookies belong in the gourmet dessert club.*

1 cup + 2 tablespoons The GF Cookie Lady's Flour (page 4)
1 (3.9-oz.) box <u>instant</u> chocolate cherry pudding/pie filling mix
2 tablespoons unsweetened cocoa powder
½ teaspoon xanthan gum
½ teaspoon baking soda
¼ teaspoon salt
¼ cup (½ stick) unsalted butter
¼ cup canola oil
⅓ cup firmly packed light brown sugar
1 teaspoon pure almond extract
½ teaspoon pure vanilla extract
1 large egg
¼ cup semisweet chocolate chips
¼ cup coarsely chopped hazelnuts (filberts)
½ cup tart dried cherries
½ cup chocolate hazelnut spread (such as Nutella®)

Cookie Tip:

 Nutella® is located in the peanut butter aisle. For a thinner consistency, add a little milk to it and microwave 10-15 seconds.

1. Preheat oven to **350° F.** Line cookie sheets with parchment paper.

2. Sift flour, dry pudding mix, cocoa powder, xanthan gum, baking soda and salt in bowl; stir. Set aside.

3. Beat butter, oil, brown sugar, almond and vanilla extracts in large mixer bowl on medium speed until well mixed, about 2 minutes. Beat in egg. Gradually beat in flour mixture. Stir in chocolate chips, nuts and dried cherries.

4. Measure dough in 2 tablespoon portions; drop 2 inches apart on prepared sheet. With lightly moistened hand, flatten dough to ½ inch thickness. Keep dough refrigerated until ready to bake.

5. Bake **9 to 11 minutes** or until centers are set. Cool 4 minutes on cookie sheet then transfer to wire rack to cool completely. **Frost** with chocolate hazelnut spread.

6. Store in airtight container up to 2 days or freeze, unfrosted, up to 2 months.

Variation:

 Frost cookies with Caramel Frosting (page 143) and garnish with finely chopped hazelnuts.

Makes 1½ dozen (3-inch) cookies

Chocolate Chip Pralines

These cookies warrant star billing in a whole repertoire of chocolate chip recipes your family will relish. You'll need to make praline pecans ahead of time before making this cookie recipe.

2¼ cups The GF Cookie Lady's Flour (page 4)
1¼ teaspoons xanthan gum
1 teaspoon baking soda
½ teaspoon salt
1 cup (2 sticks) unsalted butter
1 cup firmly packed light brown sugar
2 teaspoons pure vanilla extract
2 large eggs
1 cup semisweet chocolate chips
1½ cups coarsely chopped praline pecans (page 128)

1. Preheat oven to **350° F.** Line cookie sheets with parchment paper.

2. Sift flour, xanthan gum, baking soda and salt in bowl; stir. Set aside.

3. Beat butter, brown sugar and vanilla in large mixer bowl on medium speed until creamy, about 4 minutes. Beat in eggs, one at a time. Gradually beat in flour mixture. Stir in chocolate chips and nuts.

4. Measure dough in 2 tablespoon portions; drop 3 inches apart on prepared sheet. With hand, slightly flatten dough to ½-inch thickness.

5. Bake **11 to 13 minutes** or until light golden brown. Cool 4 minutes on cookie sheet then transfer to wire rack to cool completely.

6. Store in airtight container up to 2 days or freeze up to 2 months.

Makes 2½ dozen (2½–inch) cookies

Cookie Tips:

 Praline pecans make wonderful hostess gifts-wrapped in cellophane bag with a colorful ribbon.

 For convenience, find praline pecans in supermarkets. Read labels.

Variation:

Replace praline pecans and 1 teaspoon vanilla extract with Maple Nuts (page 128) and 1 teaspoon maple extract. Yummy!

Chocolate Crème-Filled Miniwiches

Here is a fun and quick cookie to make with kids. Your hands, not a mixer, are used to make these soft bite-size cookies. Make your favorite filling and create miniwiches. (Photo page 46)

½ cup The GF Cookie Lady's Flour (page 4)
⅛ teaspoon xanthan gum
¼ teaspoon cream of tartar
¼ teaspoon baking soda
2 large egg yolks
⅓ cup chocolate hazelnut spread (such as Nutella®)
1 recipe favorite sandwich filling (pages 137-140)

1. Preheat oven to **375° F.** Line a cookie sheet with parchment paper.

2. Sift flour, xanthan gum, cream of tartar and baking soda in bowl; stir. Set aside.

3. Combine egg yolks and chocolate hazelnut spread in another bowl. Stir in flour mixture. Dough is stiff; use hands to finish mixing.

4. Measure dough in 1 teaspoon portions; flatten between hands into 1-inch diameter circles and place 1-inch apart on prepared sheet.

5. Bake **5 minutes** or until centers are set. Do not overbake. Cool 1 minute on cookie sheet then transfer to wire rack to cool completely.

6. Make **Filling:** spread favorite filling between two cookies and make miniwiches.

7. Store in airtight container up to 3 days or freeze up to 2 months.

Makes 1½ dozen bite-size cookie sandwiches

Cookie Tips:

 Find Nutella® in the peanut butter aisle.

 Use leftover egg whites in Magical Macaroons (page 16)

Variations:

 Make one cookie and change filling to create many cookie flavors. Suggested filling flavors are: Caramel Crème, Cherry Crème, and Raspberry Crème (pages 137-140).

 Sprinkle confectioners' sugar over cookie sandwiches for a pretty presentation.

Chocolate Macaroons

My friend, Kathy, has made these family favorites every Christmas for the past 25 years. Hope you enjoy them year round.

1 (14-oz.) can sweetened condensed milk
1 (1-oz.) square unsweetened chocolate, coarsely chopped

¼ teaspoon salt
½ teaspoon pure vanilla extract
½ teaspoon pure almond extract
1 (7-oz.) package sweetened flaked coconut (equals 2⅔ cups)
½ cup coarsely chopped macadamias (optional)

1. Preheat oven to **350° F.** Line cookie sheets with parchment paper.

2. Combine sweetened condensed milk and chocolate in large microwave-safe bowl. Microwave, uncovered, on High (100 percent power) in 30 second intervals until melted. Stir after each interval. Remove from microwave; stir in salt, vanilla and almond extracts, coconut and nuts.

3. Measure dough in 1½ tablespoon portions, drop 2 inches apart on prepared sheet.

4. Bake **11 to 12 minutes** or until centers are set. Cool 2 minutes on cookie sheet then transfer to wire rack to cool completely.

5. Store in airtight container up to 3 days.

Makes 2 dozen (2-inch) cookies

Cookie Tip:

 Flaked coconut is cut into small pieces and is drier than shredded. To measure sweetened flaked coconut, lightly pack it into dry measuring cup.

Variation:

 Replace vanilla and almond extracts with peppermint extract for a minty flavor or rum extract for a tropical winner.

Chocolate-Minty Marvels

A surprising blast of peppermint wakens your taste buds as you bite into this double chocolate cookie.

¾ cup The GF Cookie Lady's Flour (page 4)
½ teaspoon xanthan gum
¼ teaspoon baking soda
½ teaspoon baking powder
¼ teaspoon salt

¼ cup (½ stick) unsalted butter
⅓ cup firmly packed light brown sugar
¼ cup granulated sugar
1 teaspoon pure vanilla extract
1 teaspoon pure peppermint extract

1 large egg
½ cup semisweet chocolate chips, melted and cooled

1½ cups chocolate mint candies, cut in small pieces; freeze

Cookie Tip:

 Find peppermint baking chips especially around the holidays. Freeze extra packages for later baking. Read labels!

Variation:

 Frost with Chocolate-Peppermint Glaze (page 145) to enhance chocolate and peppermint flavors in cookie.

1. Preheat oven to **350° F.** Line cookie sheets with parchment paper.

2. Sift flour, xanthan gum, baking soda, baking powder and salt in bowl; stir. Set aside.

3. Beat butter, brown sugar, granulated sugar, vanilla and peppermint extracts in large mixer bowl on medium speed until creamy, about 4 minutes. Beat in egg and melted chocolate. Gradually beat in flour mixture. Stir in candy pieces.

4. Measure dough in 1½ tablespoon portions; drop 3 inches apart on prepared sheet. Keep dough refrigerated until ready to bake.

5. Bake **12 to 14 minutes**. Cookies puff up in oven and flatten when cooled. Cool 5 minutes on cookie sheet then transfer to wire rack to cool completely.

6. Store in airtight container up to 2 days or freeze up to 2 months.

Makes 15 (3-inch) cookies

Chocolate Roloz

Reach into the cookie jar and snag some of these soft and chewy championship cookies. There is a little surprise inside each one; definitely a 'glass of milk' sort of cookie. (Photo page 46)

1½ cups The GF Cookie Lady's Flour (page 4)   ⅓ cup unsweetened cocoa powder   ½ teaspoon xanthan gum   ½ teaspoon baking soda   ½ teaspoon baking powder   ¼ teaspoon salt
½ cup (1 stick) unsalted butter   ½ cup firmly packed light brown sugar   ½ cup granulated sugar   1 teaspoon pure vanilla extract
2 large eggs
2 (1.7-oz.) Rolo® candy bars, cut each piece in half, then freeze

1. Sift flour, cocoa powder, xanthan gum, baking soda, baking powder and salt in bowl; stir. Set aside.

2. Beat butter, brown sugar, granulated sugar and vanilla in large mixer bowl on medium speed until creamy, about 4 minutes. Beat in eggs, one at a time. Gradually beat in flour mixture. Cover and refrigerate dough 30 minutes or until firm enough to shape into balls.

3. Preheat oven to **350° F.** Line cookie sheets with parchment paper.

4. Measure dough in 2 tablespoon portions; place <u>frozen</u> candy piece inside center of dough, making sure candy is completely covered by dough. With lightly moistened hands, shape dough into balls; place 3 inches apart on prepared sheet. Keep dough refrigerated until ready to bake.

5. Bake **13 to 14 minutes** or until centers are set and small cracks form on top. Cool 4 minutes on cookie sheet then transfer to wire rack to cool completely.

6. Store in airtight container up to 2 days or freeze up to 2 months.

Makes 1½ dozen (3-inch) cookies

Cookie Tip:

 Freezing candy pieces helps to minimize candy oozing out of cookie as it bakes.

Variation:

 For decorative appeal and nutritional value, roll balls in almond flour/meal and bake as directed.

Chocolate Surprise Balls

Double your pleasure with these simple-to-make chocolaty cookies dipped in a shiny dark chocolate glaze. A little surprise is rolled up inside!

1 cup The GF Cookie Lady's Flour (page 4) 1 teaspoon xanthan gum ⅛ teaspoon salt ¼ teaspoon ground cinnamon
1 cup semisweet chocolate chips 1½ tablespoons unsalted butter
½ (14-oz.) can sweetened condensed milk (equals ⅔ cup) ½ teaspoon pure vanilla extract
20-24 walnuts, toasted*
1 recipe Chocolate Glaze (page 145)

1. Preheat oven to **350° F.** Line cookie sheets with parchment paper.

2. Sift flour, xanthan gum, salt and cinnamon in bowl; stir. Set aside.

3. Put chocolate chips and butter in large microwave-safe bowl. Microwave, uncovered, on High (100 percent power) in 30 second intervals until melted. Stir after each interval. Remove from microwave; stir in sweetened condensed milk and vanilla. Gradually stir in flour mixture.

4. Shape 1 tablespoon of dough around each walnut. Be sure nut is completely covered by dough. Roll into balls; space 2 inches apart on prepared sheet. Keep dough refrigerated until ready to bake.

5. Bake **6 to 8 minutes** or until tops feel firm when lightly pressed. Cookies do not flatten and are greasy-looking until they set. Cool 4 minutes on cookie sheet then transfer to wire rack to cool completely.

6. **Frost.**

7. Store in airtight container up to 2 days or freeze, unfrosted, up to 2 months.

Makes almost 2 dozen (1-inch) cookies

Cookie Tips:

 *To toast walnuts: spread nuts in single layer on jelly roll pan. Bake at 325° F. 8-10 minutes. Cool before using.

 Use remaining condensed milk (⅔ cup) to make another batch of these cookies or make Almond-Coconut Cups (page 82).

Variation:

 Hide other surprises inside the dough such as raisins, ⅛ teaspoon of your favorite jam, chocolate candy kisses, or flavored nuts.

Chocolate Waffle Cookies

No need to heat your kitchen in the summer, use your waffle iron and make these yummy cookies in a flash!

1 cup The GF Cookie Lady's Flour (page 4)
¼ teaspoon xanthan gum
½ teaspoon salt
¼ teaspoon ground cinnamon
¼ cup granulated sugar

2 (1-oz.) squares semisweet chocolate, cut in pieces
½ cup unsalted butter, cut in pieces

2 large eggs
1 teaspoon pure vanilla extract

¼ cup chocolate hazelnut spread (such as Nutella®)

1. Preheat waffle iron. Do not grease.

2. Sift flour, xanthan gum, salt, cinnamon and granulated sugar in bowl; stir. Set aside.

3. Put chocolate and butter in large microwave-safe bowl. Microwave, uncovered, on High (100 percent power) in 30 second intervals until melted. Stir after each interval. Remove from microwave, stir in eggs and vanilla. Gradually stir in flour mixture.

4. Measure dough in 2 tablespoon portions; drop in center of each ungreased waffle grid. Bake 30 seconds or until centers are set. Remove cookies with fork and place on wire rack to cool completely.

5. **Frost** with chocolate hazelnut spread.

6. Store in airtight container up to 2 days or freeze, unfrosted, up to 2 months.

Makes 14 (2½-inch) cookies

Cookie Tips:

 Recipe made with regular waffle iron. If using Belgian waffle iron, some adjustments may need to be made.

 Nutella® is found in peanut butter aisle.

Variations:

 For German Chocolate Cake flavor, frost cookies with ½ recipe Fudge Frosting (page 144).

 Replace granulated sugar with vanilla-scented sugar (page 131).

Double Chocolate Delights

Wow family and friends with these double fudgy cookies topped with a chocolate buttery frosting. Easy to make and requires no mixer; they are perfect for chocoholics. (Photo page 46)

⅔ cup The GF Cookie Lady's Flour (page 4)   ½ teaspoon xanthan gum   ½ teaspoon baking powder   ¼ teaspoon salt
1 cup semisweet chocolate chips   2 (1-oz.) squares unsweetened chocolate, coarsely chopped   2 tablespoons unsalted butter
⅔ cup firmly packed light brown sugar   1 teaspoon pure vanilla extract   4 large eggs, slightly beaten
½ cup semisweet chocolate chips   4 (1.4-oz.) Heath® candy bars, coarsely chopped and <u>divided</u> (equals 1 cup)
1 recipe Chocolate Buttercream Frosting (page 143)

Cookie Tip:

 Four (1.4-oz.) Heath® candy bars equals 1 cup. Use ½ cup in dough and remaining ½ cup as garnish.

1. Preheat oven to **375° F.** Line cookie sheets with parchment paper.

2. Sift flour, xanthan gum, baking powder and salt in bowl; stir. Set aside.

3. Put 1 cup chocolate chips, chocolate squares and butter in large microwave-safe bowl. Microwave, uncovered, on High (100 percent power) in 30 second intervals until melted. Stir after each interval. Cool 5 minutes. Stir in brown sugar, vanilla and eggs. Gradually stir in flour mixture. Stir in ½ cup chocolate chips and ½ cup candy pieces.

4. Measure dough into 1½ tablespoon portions; drop 3 inches apart on prepared cookie sheet. Dough is runny, don't refrigerate.

5. Bake **10 to 12 minutes** or until centers are set. Cool 3 minutes on cookie sheet then transfer to wire rack to cool completely. Toffee bits may ooze out of cookies.

6. **Frost** and garnish with remaining candy pieces (½ cup) while frosting is still wet.

7. Store in airtight container up to 2 days or freeze, unfrosted, up to 2 months.

Makes 2½ dozen (2½-inch) cookies

Variations:

 Replace garnish with colorful candy confetti.

 Frost with Peanut Butter Buttercream Frosting (page 142).

Triple Chocolate Bliss

You will triple love these chunky gems made from fudgy dough intensified with chocolate morsels. Add buttery, rich-flavored macadamia nuts and these decadent cookies become truly blissful. (Photo page 46)

2 tablespoons The GF Cookie Lady's Flour (page 4)   ⅛ teaspoon xanthan gum   ⅛ teaspoon baking powder   ⅛ teaspoon salt
4 (1-oz.) squares semisweet chocolate, coarsely chopped   2 tablespoons unsalted butter
½ cup granulated sugar   ½ teaspoon pure vanilla extract   1 large egg
½ cup coarsely chopped macadamia nuts   ¼ cup semisweet chocolate chips   ¼ cup milk chocolate chips   ¼ cup white chocolate chips

Cookie Tip:

 That's correct, only 2 tablespoons of The GF Cookie Lady's Flour is needed.

1. Preheat oven to **350° F.** Line cookie sheets with parchment paper.

2. Sift flour, xanthan gum, baking powder and salt in bowl; add nuts and flavored chips; stir. Set aside.

3. Put chocolate squares and butter in large microwave-safe bowl. Microwave, uncovered, on High (100 percent power) in 30 second intervals until melted. Stir after each interval. Cool 5 minutes. Stir in sugar, vanilla and egg. Gradually stir in flour mixture.

4. Measure dough in 1½ tablespoon portions; drop 3 inches apart on prepared cookie sheet.

5. Bake **11 to 12 minutes** or until tops are glossy and centers are soft. Cool 4 minutes on cookie sheet then transfer to wire rack to cool completely.

6. Store in airtight container up to 2 days or freeze up to 2 months.

Makes 15 (2½-inch) cookies

Variation:

 Replace milk chocolate chips and vanilla extract with mint chocolate chips and peppermint extract for a chocolate minty flavor.

White Chocolate-Macadamia

The classic combination of white chocolate chunks and macadamia nuts is delicious packed into these soft cookies. Toffee candy adds an interesting surprise. Tasters agreed: these are the best-ever cookies. (Photo page 46)

2½ cups The GF Cookie Lady's Flour (page 4)
1 (3.3 ounce) box <u>instant</u> white chocolate pudding/pie filling mix
1 teaspoon xanthan gum
1 teaspoon baking soda
½ teaspoon salt
½ cup (1 stick) unsalted butter
½ cup canola oil
⅔ cup firmly packed light brown sugar
½ cup granulated sugar
2 teaspoons pure vanilla extract
1 teaspoon pure almond extract
2 large eggs
½ cup white chocolate chips
1 cup coarsely chopped macadamia nuts
3 (1.4-oz.) Heath® candy bars, coarsely chopped (equals ¾ cup)

Cookie Tips:

- Before turning oven off, toast a batch of your favorite nuts; cool and store for future use (page 122).

- Use <u>instant</u> vanilla pudding/pie filling if white chocolate pudding is unavailable.

- Use quality white chocolate for best results (page 48).

1. Preheat oven to **350° F.** Line cookie sheets with parchment paper.

2. Sift flour, dry pudding mix, xanthan gum, baking soda and salt in bowl; stir. Set aside.

3. Beat butter, oil, brown sugar, granulated sugar, vanilla and almond extract in large mixer bowl on medium speed until well mixed, about 2 minutes. Beat in eggs, one at a time. Gradually beat in flour mixture. Stir in white chocolate chips, nuts and candy pieces.

4. Measure dough in 1½ tablespoon portions; drop 3 inches apart on prepared cookie sheet. With hand, flatten dough to ½-inch thickness. Keep dough refrigerated until ready to bake.

5. Bake **11 to 13 minutes** or until edges are light brown and centers are set. Cool 4 minutes on cookie sheet then transfer to wire rack to cool completely.

6. Store in airtight container up to 3 days or freeze up to 2 months.

Makes 3 dozen (2½-inch) cookies

Variation:

- For chunkier texture, replace white chocolate chips with 3-ozs. premium white chocolate. Cut into desired chunks.

Fabulous Fruity 'n Spicy Cookies

Here is a section of cookies that I, for one, find impossible to resist. Fruit and spice and everything nice! That's what you'll find here. Many of the cookies are topped with decadent frostings. Yummy!

The Fruity-Filled Pinwheels have eight filling choices, creating eight flavors with just one dough. How divine! Tasters rated Lime Sugar Cookies off the chart, but my favorites are Carrot Cake Cookies and Cinnabun Swirls.

- Ambrosia Cookies 63
- Anise Aces 64
- Banana Mashies 65
- Carrot Cake Cookies 66
- Cinnabun Swirls 67
- Date Cookes 68
- Fruit Pizza Cookie 69
- Fruity-Filled Pinwheels 70
- Lemon-Poppy Whiffers 71
- Lime Sugar Cookies 72
- Lime Thumbprints 73
- Pumpkin Cheesecake Cookies 74
- Pumpkin-Chocolate Chip 75
- Strawberry Sensations 76
- Vanilla Sugar-Nutmeg Drops 77

Clockwise from upper left: Cinnabun Swirls (p. 67), Lemon-Poppy Whiffers (p. 71), Lime Thumbprints (p. 73), Fruit Pizza Cookie (p. 69) and Pumpkin Cheesecake Cookies (p. 74)

Fruit 'n Spicy Know-How

Dried fruit becomes hard as it ages. Dried fruits should be plump and moist before adding to cookie dough. If not, the fruit may take moisture from the dough and make the cookie hard once baked or the fruit may become harder inside the cookie.

To plump dried fruits, first cut into desired size with kitchen scissors. Then soak fruit in hot liquid (water, juices or liquors) 3 to 7 minutes depending on the dryness and size of the fruit. Drain the fruit and dry thoroughly with paper towels. Toss the plumped fruit with some flour mixture from the recipe before adding the fruit to the batter. Flour helps to keep the fruit separated and suspended in the batter so it doesn't sink to the bottom of the baked cookie.

When recipe calls for freshly grated citrus zest, it means removing only the colored part of the citrus, not the white area which is very bitter. Microplane® Grater is a tool found in kitchen specialty stores that works great in zesting citrus fruits.

To extract the most juice from lemons or limes, roll the fruit on the counter with your hand then microwave it for 15 to 20 seconds. This will break down the fibers inside allowing juice to flow.

Buy the best spices you can afford in small quantities. Taste test spices for quality; they should taste spicy-sweet, not astringent and bitter. Keep in cool, dark, dry place and write date of purchase on the containers. If distinctive aroma has diminished and taste is bitter, discard and buy fresh ones. I like Penzeys Spices for the quality and price (Resources page 164).

Spices come in ground or freshly grated. Of all the spices, nutmeg is one that should be used freshly grated whenever possible—it is much more flavorful than ground and easy to produce with a grater. Nutmeg comes in small hard shells and may be purchased at kitchen specialty stores. Find a grater tool such as the Microplane® in the same location. Either ground or freshly grated may be used, but nothing compares to the spicy-sweet flavor of freshly grated nutmeg.

For Best Results:

- Read entire recipe to ensure necessary ingredients and equipment are on hand or if any advance procedure needs to be done.
- Have **all** ingredients at room temperature. Use quality ingredients.
- Preheat the oven at least 15 minutes. Keep ovenproof thermometer inside oven to ensure accurate temperature.
- Measure accurately and mix according to directions. Scrape bowl often to ensure homogenous dough.
- Use spring-release cookie scoop for uniform size that bakes evenly and at same time.
- Bake one cookie sheet at a time on the middle rack of the oven. Use quality cookie sheets.
- Check cookies at the minimum baking time; continue baking, if necessary, in one-minute intervals. Every oven bakes a little differently. Bake one "test" cookie to gauge baking time in your oven. Better to underbake than overbake.

Ambrosia Cookies

Loaded with dried fruit, coconut, walnuts and gluten-free oats, these wholesome cookies are real pleasers.

1 cup The GF Cookie Lady's Flour (page 4)   ½ teaspoon xanthan gum   ½ teaspoon baking powder   ½ teaspoon baking soda   ½ teaspoon salt   ½ teaspoon ground cinnamon
½ cup (1 stick) unsalted butter   ½ cup firmly packed light brown sugar   ½ cup granulated sugar   1 teaspoon freshly grated orange zest   1 teaspoon pure vanilla extract
1 large egg
¾ cup gluten-free oats   ½ cup sweetened flaked coconut   ½ cup raisins   ½ cup dates, cut into pieces   ½ cup coarsely chopped walnuts

Cookie Tips:

 See Resource page 163 to find gluten-free oats.

 Use kitchen scissors to cut dates easier. Spray scissors with vegetable cooking spray to prevent fruit from sticking.

1. Preheat oven to **375°F**. Line cookie sheets with parchment paper.

2. Sift flour, xanthan gum, baking powder, baking soda, salt and cinnamon in bowl; stir. Set aside.

3. Beat butter, brown sugar, granulated sugar, orange zest and vanilla in large mixer bowl on medium speed until creamy, about 4 minutes. Beat in egg. Gradually beat in flour mixture. Beat in oats, coconut, raisins, dates and nuts.

4. Measure dough in 1½ tablespoon portions; drop 3 inches apart on prepared sheet.

5. Bake **11 to 13 minutes** or until edges are brown and centers are slightly moist. Cool 4 minutes on cookie sheet then transfer to wire rack to cool completely.

6. Store in airtight container up to 2 days or freeze up to 2 months.

Makes almost 2 dozen (3-inch) cookies

Variation:

If gluten-free oats are not in your diet, replace with 1 cup quinoa flakes. Find in health-related grocery stores.

Anise Aces

If you like the bold flavor of licorice; these soft cookies are aces for you.
Pine nuts provide extra crunch and visual appeal.

1¼ cups The GF Cookie Lady's Flour (page 4)   1 teaspoon xanthan gum   ¼ teaspoon salt   2½ teaspoons <u>ground</u> anise seeds
½ cup (1 stick) unsalted butter   ⅔ cup granulated sugar   1 teaspoon pure vanilla extract   1 tablespoon freshly grated lemon zest (1 large lemon)
1 large egg
2 tablespoons pine nuts

1. Preheat oven to **350° F.** Line cookie sheets with parchment paper.

2. Sift flour, xanthan gum, salt and anise in bowl; stir. Set aside.

3. Beat butter, granulated sugar, vanilla and lemon zest in large mixer bowl on medium speed until creamy, about 4 minutes. Beat in egg. Gradually beat in flour mixture.

4. Measure dough in 1½ tablespoon portions; shape into balls and drop 3 inches apart on prepared sheet. With hand, slightly flatten dough to ¼-inch thick and press 2-3 pine nuts on top. If dough is sticky, refrigerate 30 minutes.

5. Bake **11 to 13 minutes** or until edges are lightly browned. Cool 3 minutes on cookie sheet then transfer to wire rack to cool completely.

6. Store in airtight container up to 2 days or freeze up to 2 months.

Makes 2 dozen (3-inch) cookies

Cookie Tip:

 Dough may be shaped into 2 log rolls, wrapped securely in plastic wrap, refrigerated and baked later. Cut each log crosswise into ¼-⅜-inch thick slices; bake as directed.

Variations:

 Frost with Anise Buttercream Frosting (page 143).

 For Anise Fig Aces: add ½ teaspoon ground cinnamon and ¼ cup finely chopped dried figs. Replace pine nuts with walnut halves.

Banana Mashies

Filled with nuts, fruit and gluten-free oats, this cookie could be the start of a new breakfast trend. It was a definite smash with the taste testers.

1¼ cups The GF Cookie Lady's Flour (page 4) ½ teaspoon xanthan gum ½ teaspoon baking soda ½ teaspoon salt 1 teaspoon ground cinnamon
6 tablespoons solid vegetable shortening 1 cup granulated sugar ½ teaspoon pure vanilla extract ½ teaspoon rum extract (optional)
1 large egg ½ cup mashed bananas (about 7-inch banana)
¾ cup gluten-free oats* ¼ cup raisins ¼ cup coarsely chopped walnuts

1. Preheat oven to **375° F.** Line cookie sheets with parchment paper.

2. Sift flour, xanthan gum, baking soda, salt and cinnamon in bowl; stir. Set aside.

3. Beat shortening, granulated sugar, vanilla and rum extracts in large mixer bowl on medium speed until mixed, about 2 minutes. Beat in egg and banana. Gradually beat in flour mixture. Beat in oats, raisins and nuts.

4. Measure dough in 1½ tablespoon portions; drop 3 inches apart on prepared sheet.

5. Bake **12 to 14 minutes** or until golden brown. Cool 3 minutes on cookie sheet then transfer to wire rack to cool completely.

6. Store in airtight container up to 3 days or freeze up to 2 months.

Makes 1½ dozen (2½-inch) cookies

Cookie Tips:

 *Find suppliers for gluten-free oats in Resources page 163.

 Raisins and bananas are rich in vitamin C and potassium; walnuts are high in cancer-fighting antioxidants.

Variation:

 If gluten-free oats are not in your diet, substitute with quinoa flakes. Find quinoa flakes in health related grocery stores.

Fabulous Fruity 'n Spicy Cookies

Carrot Cake Cookies

Everyone will love these cookies. Put on the coffee pot; and have friends over for cookies, coffee and great conversation.

1¼ cups The GF Cookie Lady's Flour (page 4)
½ (3.4-oz.) box <u>instant</u> vanilla pudding/pie filling mix
½ teaspoon xanthan gum
¾ teaspoon baking powder
½ teaspoon baking soda
¼ teaspoon salt
1 teaspoon ground cinnamon
¼ cup (½ stick) unsalted butter
¼ cup canola oil
⅓ cup firmly packed light brown sugar
¼ cup granulated sugar
1 teaspoon pure vanilla extract
1 large egg plus 1 large yolk
1 (8-oz.) can crushed pineapple, very well drained
¼ cup grated carrots
¼ cup raisins
¼ cup coarsely chopped walnuts
¼ cup sweetened flaked coconut
1 recipe Pineapple Cream Cheese Frosting (page 142)

Cookie Tips:

 ½ (3.4 oz) box of <u>instant</u> dry pudding mix is equal to 5 tablespoons.

 Squeeze pineapple with hands until ¼ cup packed pineapple remains. Too much moisture in the cookies will make them soggy. Save 1-2 tablespoons of juice for frosting.

Variation:

 Replace grated carrots with unpeeled shredded zucchini for extra fiber.

1. Preheat oven to **350° F.** Line cookie sheets with parchment paper.

2. Sift flour, dry pudding mix, xanthan gum, baking powder, baking soda, salt and cinnamon in bowl; stir. Set aside.

3. Beat butter, oil, brown sugar, granulated sugar and vanilla in large mixer bowl on medium speed until well mixed, about 2 minutes. Beat in egg and egg yolk. Gradually beat in flour mixture. Beat in well drained pineapple, carrots, raisins, walnuts and coconut.

4. Measure dough in 2 tablespoon portions; drop 3 inches apart on prepared sheet. Keep dough refrigerated until ready to bake.

5. Bake **12 to 15 minutes** or until golden brown. Cool 3 minutes on cookie sheet then transfer to wire rack to cool completely.

6. **Frost.**

7. Refrigerate cookies in airtight container up to 3 days or freeze, unfrosted, up to 2 months.

Makes 3½ dozen (2½-inch) cookies

Cinnabun Swirls

Cinnamon swirl cookies look and taste like little cinnamon rolls. Drizzle with vanilla glaze, they're sure to please. (Photo page 60)

2 cups The GF Cookie Lady's Flour (page 4)
1½ teaspoons xanthan gum
½ teaspoon baking soda
¼ teaspoon salt
¼ cup (½ stick) unsalted butter
¼ cup solid vegetable shortening
½ cup firmly packed light brown sugar
½ cup granulated sugar
1 teaspoon pure vanilla extract
2 large eggs
¼ cup granulated sugar
1 tablespoon ground cinnamon
¼ teaspoon vanilla powder* (optional)
1 recipe Vanilla Glaze (page 146)

Cookie Tips:

 Slice dough the same thickness so cookies will bake evenly and in the same amount of time.

 A bench scraper is a useful tool to both slice and transfer dough to cookie sheet (page 7).

 *Find vanilla powder in health-related or specialty shops (Resources page 162).

Variation:

 Replace cinnamon with pumpkin spice or apple spice.

1. Sift flour, xanthan gum, baking soda and salt in bowl; stir. Set aside.

2. Beat butter, shortening, brown sugar, granulated sugar and vanilla in large mixer bowl on medium speed until creamy, about 3 minutes. Beat in eggs, one at a time. Gradually beat in flour mixture.

3. Combine ¼ cup granulated sugar, cinnamon and vanilla powder in small bowl.

4. Divide dough in half. Roll half of dough between 2 sheets of plastic wrap into 10-inch circle about ¼-inch thick. Remove top sheet of plastic; sprinkle and lightly press 2 tablespoons of cinnamon sugar over dough to within ½-inch of edges. Roll up, using plastic to lift and guide the roll. Pinch ends to seal; wrap in plastic. Repeat with remaining dough. Refrigerate at least 1 hour or until firm enough to slice.

5. Preheat oven to **350° F.** Line cookie sheets with parchment paper.

6. Cut dough into ½-inch slices; place 2 inches apart on prepared sheet. Bake **12 to 13 minutes** or until edges are lightly browned. Cool 2 minutes on cookie sheet then transfer to wire rack to cool completely. **Frost**.

7. Store in airtight container up to 2 days or freeze, unfrosted, up to 2 months.

Makes almost 3 dozen (2½-inch) cookies

Date Cookies

Make a 'date' with these cookies and be glad you did!

```
2 cups The GF Cookie Lady's Flour (page 4)
½ teaspoon xanthan gum
½ teaspoon baking soda
½ teaspoon baking powder
¼ teaspoon salt

½ cup (1 stick) unsalted butter
½ cup firmly packed light brown sugar
½ cup granulated sugar
1 teaspoon pure vanilla extract
½ teaspoon pure almond extract

2 large eggs
1½ teaspoons water

1½ cups dates, cut in small pieces
```

Cookie Tips:

 Use kitchen scissors to cut dates easier.

 Dates are high in flavor, fiber and nutrients especially calcium, potassium and phosphorus.

1. Preheat oven to **350° F.** Line cookie sheets with parchment paper.
2. Sift flour, xanthan gum, baking soda, baking powder and salt in bowl; stir. Set aside.
3. Beat butter, brown sugar, granulated sugar, vanilla and almond extracts in large mixer bowl on medium speed until creamy, about 4 minutes. Beat in eggs, one at a time, and water. Gradually beat in flour mixture. Stir in dates.
4. Measure dough in 1½ tablespoon portions; drop 3 inches apart on prepared sheets.
5. Bake **11 to 12 minutes** or until edges are lightly browned. Cool 2 minutes on cookie sheet then transfer to wire rack to cool completely.
6. Store in airtight container up to 2 days or freeze up to 2 months.

Makes 2 dozen (2½-inch) cookies

Variations:

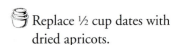 Replace ½ cup dates with dried apricots.

 Replace dates with dried figs.

Fruit Pizza Cookie

*Get ready for a slice of scrumptious fruit pizza.
Three toppings are given to show you the versatility of this cookie. Get creative! (Photo page 60)*

1 cup The GF Cookie Lady's Flour (page 4) ½ teaspoon xanthan gum ¼ teaspoon salt
2 tablespoons solid vegetable shortening 2 tablespoons canola oil ⅓ cup granulated sugar 1 teaspoon pure vanilla extract ½ teaspoon pure almond extract
1 large egg yolk 1½ teaspoons water

1. Preheat oven to **350° F.** Spray two (9-inch) fluted tart pans (removable bottom) with vegetable cooking spray.

2. Sift flour, xanthan gum and salt in bowl; stir. Set aside.

3. Beat shortening, oil, granulated sugar, vanilla and almond extracts in large mixer bowl on medium speed until mixed, about 1 minute. Beat in egg yolk and water. Gradually beat in flour mixture.

4. Divide dough into two equal portions. With lightly moistened fingers, press dough in bottom and ¼ inch up on sides of each prepared pan.

5. Bake **12 to 13 minutes** or until edges are lightly browned. Cool in pan on wire rack.

6. Spread favorite topping over crust (see sidebar).

7. Refrigerate cookies in airtight container up to 3 days. Freeze crust (without toppings) up to 2 months.

Makes almost 2 dozen slices

Variations:

 Toppings #1:
Beat 2 ounces (4 tablespoons) cream cheese at room temperature, ¼ cup granulated sugar and 1 teaspoon vanilla extract with electric handheld mixer until smooth. Stir in ⅔ cup Cool Whip®. Spread topping on cooled crust. Top with favorite fruits such as sliced strawberries, halved grapes, slice kiwi or pineapple chunks. Topping is enough for 2 tarts.

 Topping #2:
Make your favorite instant pudding (use 1¾ cups milk, instead of 2 cups) and spread on top of cooled crust. Top with sliced bananas, coconut and chocolate chips. Topping is enough for 2 tart pans.

 Topping #3:
Purchase gluten-free lemon curd and spread on cooled crust. Top with fresh blueberries and toasted, chopped pecans. Find lemon curd in baking aisles of most supermarkets.

Fruity-Filled Pinwheels

These cookies have eight filling choices, creating eight flavors with just one dough. How divine!

2 cups The GF Cookie Lady's Flour (page 4)   1½ teaspoons xanthan gum   ½ teaspoon baking soda   ¼ teaspoon salt
¼ cup (½ stick) unsalted butter   ¼ cup solid vegetable shortening   ½ cup firmly packed light brown sugar   ½ cup granulated sugar   1 teaspoon pure vanilla extract
2 large eggs
1 recipe favorite fruit filling (page 134-136)

Cookie Tips:

- Log rolls cut in ¼-inch thickness will bake into thin, crisp cookies; those cut in ½-inch or more thickness result in thicker, chewier ones. Note: thin slices are more difficult to slice and bake faster.

- Cookie fillings should be thick enough to keep their consistency in the heat of the oven or they will ooze out.

1. Make **Filling**.

2. Sift flour, xanthan gum, baking soda and salt in bowl; stir. Set aside.

3. Beat butter, shortening, brown sugar, granulated sugar and vanilla in large mixer bowl on medium speed until creamy, about 3 minutes. Beat in eggs, one at a time. Gradually beat in flour mixture.

4. Divide dough in half. Roll half of dough between 2 sheets of plastic wrap into 10-inch circle about ¼-inch thick. Remove top sheet of plastic. Spread ⅓ to ½ cup filling over dough to within 1-inch of edges. Roll up, using plastic to lift and guide the roll. Pinch ends to seal; wrap in foil. Repeat with remaining dough and filling. Refrigerate at least 1 hour or until firm enough to slice.

5. Preheat oven to **350° F**. Line cookie sheets with parchment paper.

6. Cut dough into ½-inch slices; place 2 inches apart on prepared sheet. Bake **12 to 13 minutes** or until edges are lightly browned. Cool 2 minutes on cookie sheet then transfer to wire rack to cool completely.

7. Store in airtight container up to 3 days or freeze up to 2 months.

Makes 2 dozen (3-inch) cookies

Lemon-Poppy Whiffers

A chewy dense cookie filled with poppy seeds, fragrant spices, and a whiff of lemon makes for great milk or coffee dunking. (Photo page 60)

2½ cups The GF Cookie Lady's Flour (page 4) 1½ teaspoons xanthan gum 2 teaspoons baking powder 1 teaspoon baking soda ½ teaspoon salt 2 teaspoons poppy seeds ½ teaspoon ground cardamom 1 teaspoon ground cinnamon
½ cup (1 stick) unsalted butter, melted and cooled 1 cup granulated sugar ¼ cup light corn syrup 2 tablespoons freshly grated lemon zest (1 large lemon) 1 teaspoon pure almond extract ½ teaspoon pure lemon oil*
1 large egg, slightly beaten
½ cup raisins (optional)
1 recipe Lemon Glaze (page 146)

Cookie Tips:

 *Find pure lemon oil in kitchen specialty stores (Resources page 164). Or use 1 teaspoon of lemon extract.

 For pretty presentation, garnish glazed cookies with freshly grated lemon zest.

Variation:

 Replace raisins with finely chopped dates.

1. Preheat oven to **325° F.** Line cookie sheets with parchment paper.

2. Sift flour, xanthan gum, baking powder, baking soda, salt, poppy seeds, cardamom and cinnamon in bowl; stir. Set aside.

3. Combine melted butter, granulated sugar, corn syrup, lemon zest, almond extract and lemon oil in large bowl. Stir in egg. Gradually stir in flour mixture. Use hands to finish mixing. Stir in raisins, if desired.

4. Measure dough in 1½ tablespoon portions; drop 3 inches apart on prepared sheet. With hand, slightly flatten dough to ¼-inch thickness.

5. Bake **11 to 12 minutes** or until edges are lightly browned. Cool 3 minutes on cookie sheet then transfer to wire rack to cool completely.

6. **Frost.**

7. Store in airtight container up to 2 days or freeze, unfrosted, up to 2 months.

Makes 2 dozen (3-inch) cookies

Lime Sugar Cookies

*This cookie was a celebrity among taste testers and voted as one of the best!
Double the recipe for double the pleasure!*

1½ cups The GF Cookie Lady's Flour (page 4)
1¼ teaspoons xanthan gum
1 teaspoon cream of tartar
½ teaspoon baking soda
¼ teaspoon salt
½ cup (1 stick) unsalted butter
1 cup citrus-scented sugar–lime (page 130)
¼ teaspoon pure lime oil*
1 large egg

Cookie Tips:

 Use more freshly grated lime zest for a stronger lime flavor.

 *Find pure lime oil in kitchen specialty stores (Resources page 164).

1. Preheat oven to **350° F.** Line cookie sheets with parchment paper.

2. Sift flour, xanthan gum, cream of tartar, baking soda and salt in bowl; stir. Set aside.

3. Beat butter, lime-scented sugar and lime oil in large mixer bowl on medium speed until creamy, about 4 minutes. Beat in egg. Gradually beat in flour mixture.

4. Measure dough in 1½ tablespoon portions; shape into balls. Place balls 3 inches apart on prepared sheet. With hand, slightly flatten dough to ½-inch thickness.

5. Bake **13 to 14 minutes** or until edges are lightly browned. Cool 3 minutes on cookie sheet then transfer to wire rack to cool completely. Sprinkle lime-scented sugar over cookies, if desired.

6. Store in airtight container up to 2 days or freeze up to 2 months.

Makes 1½ dozen (3-inch) cookies

Variation:

 If lime is not a favorite flavor, try orange or lemon for an equally awesome cookie.

Lime Thumbprints

These attractive cookies with a dab of lime curd nestled in a buttery cookie base are a perfect addition to any dessert tray. (Photo page 60)

2½ cups The GF Cookie Lady's Flour (page 4)   2 teaspoons xanthan gum   ½ teaspoon baking powder   ¼ teaspoon salt   ½ teaspoon freshly grated nutmeg   ¼ teaspoon ground cinnamon
1 cup (2 sticks) unsalted butter   ¾ cup citrus-scented sugar–lime (page 130)   2 teaspoons pure vanilla extract   1 teaspoon pure lime oil*
2 large egg yolks
¼ cup lime curd (see cookie tip)

1. Sift flour, xanthan gum, baking powder, salt, nutmeg and cinnamon in bowl; stir. Set aside.

2. Beat butter, lime-scented sugar, vanilla and lime oil in large mixer bowl on medium speed until creamy, about 4 minutes. Beat in egg yolks. Gradually beat in flour mixture. Cover and refrigerate dough at least 1 hour or until firm enough to shape into balls.

3. Preheat oven to **375° F.** Line cookie sheets with parchment paper.

4. Measure dough in 1½ tablespoon portions; shape into balls and place 3 inches apart on prepared sheet. With thumb, make indentation in center of each ball. Put ½ teaspoon of lime curd into each thumbprint.

5. Bake **12 to 13 minutes** or until edges are lightly browned. Cool 3 minutes on cookie sheet then transfer to wire rack to cool completely. Sprinkle confectioners' sugar over cookies, if desired.

6. Refrigerate cookies in airtight container up to 3 days.

Makes 2 dozen (2-inch) cookies

Cookie Tips:

 *Find pure lime oil in kitchen specialty stores (Resources page 164).

 Find lime curd in baking aisle. Read labels.

Variations:

 After rolling dough into balls, dip them in egg white wash and roll in finely chopped nuts. To make egg white wash: Whisk 1 large egg white, 2 teaspoons of cold water, ⅛ teaspoon salt and 2 teaspoons granulated sugar.

 Substitute apricot preserves, granulated sugar and almond extract for lime curd, lime sugar and lime oil.

Fabulous Fruity 'n Spicy Cookies

Pumpkin Cheesecake Cookies

This cookie is a five star winner. Don't let all the ingredients discourage you from making this outstanding cookie. They will disappear in record-breaking time! (Photo page 60)

2½ cups The GF Cookie Lady's Flour (page 4)
1 (3.4-oz.) box <u>instant</u> cheesecake pudding/pie filling
1 teaspoon xanthan gum
1 teaspoon baking soda
¼ teaspoon salt
2 teaspoons ground cinnamon
¼ teaspoon ground ginger
¼ teaspoon ground cloves
¼ teaspoon freshly grated nutmeg
⅓ cup solid vegetable shortening
1 cup firmly packed light brown sugar
2 teaspoons pure vanilla extract
2 large eggs
1 (15-oz.) can 100% pure pumpkin (reserve 1 tablespoon for frosting)
1 cup dried cranberries or raisins
½ cup sweetened flaked coconut
½ cup coarsely chopped walnuts
1 recipe Pumpkin Cream Cheese Frosting (page 142)

1. Preheat oven to **350° F.** Line cookie sheets with parchment paper.
2. Sift flour, dry pudding mix, xanthan gum, baking soda, salt, cinnamon, ginger, cloves and nutmeg in bowl; stir. Set aside.
3. Beat shortening, brown sugar and vanilla in large mixer bowl on medium speed until mixed, about 1 minute. Beat in eggs, one at a time, and pumpkin. Gradually beat in flour mixture. Stir in cranberries, coconut and nuts.
4. Measure dough in 2 tablespoon portions; drop 2 inches apart on prepared sheet. With lightly moistened fingertips, flatten dough to ½-inch thickness.
5. Bake **15 to 16 minutes** or until centers are set. Cookies puff in oven and do not spread. Cool 3 minutes on cookie sheet then transfer to wire rack to cool completely. **Frost.**
6. Refrigerate cookies in airtight container up to 2 days or freeze, unfrosted, up to 2 months.

Makes 3 dozen (2-inch) cookies

Cookie Tips:

Instant cheesecake pudding/pie filling mix is popular around holidays. If unavailable, substitute <u>instant</u> vanilla pudding/pie filling mix.

Find cans of 100% pure pumpkin in baking aisle.

Variation:

Frost cookies with Vanilla Cream Cheese Frosting (page 142); garnish with toasted walnuts.

Pumpkin-Chocolate Chip

Who could resist these moist, soft and healthy cookies? Pumpkin has vitamin A and chocolate antioxidants. Pour yourself a glass of milk and enjoy these nutritious cookies.

2 cups The GF Cookie Lady's Flour (page 4) 1 teaspoon xanthan gum ½ teaspoon baking powder ½ teaspoon baking soda ¼ teaspoon salt 1 teaspoon ground cinnamon
½ cup (1 stick) unsalted butter 1½ cups firmly packed light brown sugar 2 teaspoons pure vanilla extract
1 large egg ½ (15-oz.) can 100% pure pumpkin (equals 1 cup)
1 cup semisweet chocolate chips

Cookie Tips:

 Find 100% pure pumpkin in baking aisle.

 For no leftover pumpkin, double the recipe!

1. Preheat oven to **350° F.** Line cookie sheets with parchment paper.
2. Sift flour, xanthan gum, baking powder, baking soda, salt and cinnamon in bowl; stir. Set aside.
3. Beat butter, brown sugar and vanilla in large mixer bowl on medium speed until creamy, about 4 minutes. Beat in egg and pumpkin. Gradually beat in flour mixture. Stir in chocolate chips.
4. Measure dough in 2 tablespoon portions; drop 3 inches apart on prepared sheet. Keep dough refrigerated until ready to bake.
5. Bake **15 to 16 minutes** or until golden brown. Cool 4 minutes on cookie sheet then transfer to wire rack to cool completely.
6. Store in airtight container up to 3 days or freeze up to 2 months.

Makes almost 3 dozen (2½-inch) cookies

Variation:

 Use remaining ½ can (almost 1 cup) pumpkin. Replace chocolate chips with ¾ cup white chocolate chips and ¼ cup coarsely chopped walnuts.

Fabulous Fruity 'n Spicy Cookies

Strawberry Sensations

Jam-packed with lots of strawberry flavor, this soft cookie topped with a walnut is sure to satisfy the berry enthusiast.

2½ cups The GF Cookie Lady's Flour (page 4)
1 (3.4 oz.) box <u>instant</u> strawberry pudding/pie filling mix
2 teaspoons xanthan gum
1 teaspoon baking powder
1 teaspoon baking soda
½ teaspoon salt
1 teaspoon ground cinnamon
½ cup (1 stick) unsalted butter
½ cup solid vegetable shortening
½ cup firmly packed light brown sugar
½ cup granulated sugar
1 teaspoon pure vanilla extract
½ teaspoon pure almond extract
½ teaspoon pure peppermint extract
2 large eggs
1 cup dried strawberries, cut into small pieces

Cookie Tips:

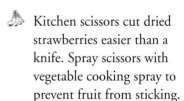

- Kitchen scissors cut dried strawberries easier than a knife. Spray scissors with vegetable cooking spray to prevent fruit from sticking.

- Find solid vegetable shortening in baking aisle.

1. Preheat oven to **350°F**. Line cookie sheets with parchment paper.

2. Sift flour, dry pudding mix, xanthan gum, baking powder, baking soda, salt and cinnamon in bowl; stir. Set aside.

3. Beat butter, shortening, brown sugar, granulated sugar, vanilla, almond and peppermint extracts in large mixer bowl on medium speed until creamy, about 4 minutes. Beat in eggs, one at a time. Gradually beat in flour mixture. Stir in dried strawberries.

4. Measure dough in 1½ tablespoon portions; drop 3 inches apart on prepared sheet. Keep dough refrigerated until ready to bake.

5. Bake **12 to 13 minutes** or until lightly browned. Cool 3 minutes on cookie sheet then transfer to wire racks to cool completely.

6. Store in airtight container for up to 2 days or freeze up to 2 months.

Makes 3 dozen (2 ½-inch) cookies

Variation:

Replace pudding with strawberry banana pudding/pie filling mix and omit peppermint extract.

Vanilla Sugar-Nutmeg Drops

Vanilla and freshly grated nutmeg make a great combination for this tender, soft cookie. Smear your favorite frosting on top and you'll want more than one!

2⅔ cups The GF Cookie Lady's Flour (page 4) 1½ teaspoons xanthan gum 1 teaspoon baking powder ½ teaspoon salt 2 teaspoons freshly grated nutmeg
¾ cup (1½ sticks) unsalted butter 1 cup vanilla-scented sugar (page 131) 2 teaspoons pure vanilla extract
2 large eggs
1 recipe Vanilla Cream Cheese Frosting (page 142)

1. Preheat oven to **400° F.** Line cookie sheets with parchment paper.
2. Sift flour, xanthan gum, baking powder, salt and nutmeg in bowl; stir. Set aside.
3. Beat butter, vanilla-scented sugar and vanilla in large mixer bowl on medium speed until creamy, about 4 minutes. Beat in eggs, one at a time. Gradually beat in flour mixture.
4. Measure dough in 1½ tablespoon portions; drop 3 inches apart on prepared sheet.
5. Bake **9 to 11 minutes** or until edges are lightly browned. Do not overbake. Cool 4 minutes on cookie sheet then transfer to wire rack to cool completely.
6. **Frost.**
7. Store in airtight container up to 2 days or freeze, unfrosted, up to 2 months.

Makes 2½ dozen (2-inch) cookies

Cookie Tip:

 Ground nutmeg may be used; but freshly grated nutmeg is the secret ingredient and makes these cookies special.

Variations:

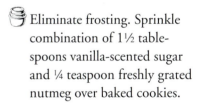 Eliminate frosting. Sprinkle combination of 1½ tablespoons vanilla-scented sugar and ¼ teaspoon freshly grated nutmeg over baked cookies.

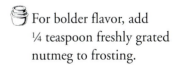 For bolder flavor, add ¼ teaspoon freshly grated nutmeg to frosting.

Naturally Nutty Cookies

Select your favorite nut: almonds, cashews, macadamias, pistachios, or walnuts. Now select a cookie recipe to match your favorite nut. What are you waiting for? Bake away! My husband's favorites are Orange-Glazed Walnut Cookies and Almond-Toffee Temptations while the tasters overwhelming voted for Almond-Coconut Cups and crunchy Walnut-Chocolate Chip Biscotti.

- Almond-Toffee Temptations 81
- Almond-Coconut Cups 82
- Caramel-Cashew Cookies 83
- Coconut Mounds 84
- Lacy Almond Cookies 85
- Lemon-Pistachio Cookies 86
- Mango-Macadamia Cookies 87
- Orange-Glazed Walnut Cookies 88
- Pistachio-Cranberry Cookies 89
- Spicy Maple Nut 90
- Walnut-Chocolate Chip Biscotti 91

Clockwise from upper left:
Lacy Almond Cookies (p. 85), Caramel-Cashew Cookies (p. 83), Almond-Coconut Cups (p. 82), Walnut-Chocolate Chip Biscotti (p. 91) and Orange-Glazed Walnut Cookies (p. 88)

Nutty Know-How:

Nuts are one of the best sources of plant protein, good fat and dietary fiber. They are nutritional powerhouses in vitamins such as folic acid, niacin, vitamins E and B, and minerals such as selenium, phosphorous and potassium. For example, almonds are high in calcium, pistachios in potassium, walnuts in an essential omega-3 fatty acid and hazelnuts (filberts) in vitamin A. The key is portion control.

New crops of nuts appear in supermarkets from October to December, so autumn is a good time to buy a year's supply. Nuts should never be stored in tin or metal containers because the metal accelerates their deterioration. Package nuts in tightly sealed heavy-duty freezer bags; freeze up to one year. Defrost nuts before baking with them.

Nuts become rancid easily. Always taste nuts before using them in the recipe to make sure they aren't rancid. Rancid nuts are easy to identify—bitter and stale flavor with no sweetness. If nuts taste slightly rancid or old, discard them.

Buy whole shelled nuts (with the shells already removed) because they have a longer shelf-life than chopped or ground nuts. Buy them whole and chop or grind them yourself for freshest results. To grind small batches of nuts, invest in an inexpensive coffee grinder found in specialty kitchen or department stores. Grinding or chopping whole nuts as you need them will reduce the chance of nuts going rancid.

Substitute flavored nuts for any recipe that calls for nuts. They are very versatile, add a flavorful dimension to baked goods and are easy to make (page 127).

Toasted nuts are tastier and crunchier than raw ones and add extra flavor and crunch to cookies. If recipe calls for nuts, toast them and taste the difference in your cookies. To save time, toast large batches of nuts; cool and store in plastic bags in the freezer for future use (page 122).

Four ounces of nuts is the equivalent of 1 cup chopped nuts.

For Best Results:

- Read entire recipe to ensure necessary ingredients and equipment are on hand or if any advance procedure needs to be done.

- Have **all** ingredients at room temperature. Use quality ingredients.

- Preheat the oven at least 15 minutes. Keep ovenproof thermometer inside oven to ensure accurate temperature.

- Measure accurately and mix according to directions. Scrape bowl often to ensure homogenous dough.

- Use spring-release cookie scoop for uniform size that bakes evenly and at same time.

- Bake one cookie sheet at a time on the middle rack of the oven. Use quality cookie sheets.

- Check cookies at the minimum baking time; continue baking, if necessary, in one-minute intervals. Every oven bakes a little differently. Bake one "test" cookie to gauge baking time in **your** oven. Better to underbake than overbake.

Almond-Toffee Temptations

Love toffee candy? Then you're sure to love these chewy, crunchy cookies, which boast lots of them. Cinnamon Almond Butter adds a surprising flavor and makes these cookies ever so tempting!

2¼ cups The GF Cookie Lady's Flour (page 4)
½ teaspoon xanthan gum
1 teaspoon baking soda
1 teaspoon baking powder
¼ teaspoon salt
¼ cup (½ stick) unsalted butter
¼ cup solid vegetable shortening
1¼ cups firmly packed light brown sugar
1 teaspoon pure vanilla extract
1 teaspoon pure almond extract
1 large egg
¼ cup Cinnamon-Almond Butter (page 124)
1 (8-oz.) package milk chocolate toffee bits, <u>divided</u>
1 recipe Almond Buttercream Frosting (page 143)

1. Make Cinnamon Almond Butter.

2. Preheat oven to **375° F.** Line cookie sheets with parchment paper.

3. Sift flour, xanthan gum, baking soda, baking powder and salt in bowl; stir. Set aside.

4. Beat butter, shortening, brown sugar, vanilla and almond extracts in large mixer bowl on medium speed until creamy, about 4 minutes. Beat in egg and cinnamon almond butter. Gradually beat in flour mixture. Beat in 1 cup toffee bits.

5. Measure dough in 1½ tablespoons portions; drop 3 inches apart on prepared sheet. With lightly moistened hand, flatten dough to ½-inch thickness. Keep dough refrigerated until ready bake.

6. Bake **9 to 11 minutes** or until edges are lightly browned. Cool 5 minutes on cookie sheet then transfer to wire rack to cool completely.

7. **Frost** and garnish with remaining toffee bits (½ cup).

8. Store in airtight container up to 2 days or freeze, unfrosted, up to 2 months.

Makes almost 3 dozen (3-inch) cookies

Cookie Tip:

Make Cinnamon-Almond Butter (page 124) in advance and refrigerate up to 2 weeks or freeze up to 2 months. Use at room temperature.

Variation:

 Eliminate frosting and candy topping for an equally awesome cookie.

Almond-Coconut Cups

If you like Almond Joy® candy bars, you will love these bite-size cookie cups. (Photo page 78)

1 cup Cookie Lady's GF Flour (page 4) ½ teaspoon xanthan gum 1 tablespoon granulated sugar ¼ teaspoon salt
½ cup (1 stick) unsalted butter 3-ozs. (⅓ cup) cream cheese
½ cup sweetened flaked coconut ½ cup almond flour/meal* ½ (14-oz.) can sweetened condensed milk (equals ⅔ cup) 1 teaspoon pure almond extract
24 chocolate candy kisses
1 recipe Chocolate Glaze (page 145)

Cookie Tips:

- *Buy almond flour/meal at health related grocery stores or pulverize ¼ cup whole raw almonds in food processor 1 minute, or until finely ground.

- A wire whisk works great for drizzling glaze over cookies. Dip whisk into glaze and shake it over cookies.

- Double this recipe or use the remaining ½ can (⅔ cup) of condensed milk to make Chocolate Surprise Balls (page 55).

1. Sift flour, xanthan gum, granulated sugar and salt in bowl; stir. Set aside.

2. Beat butter and cream cheese in large mixer bowl on medium speed until creamy, about 2 minutes. Gradually beat in flour mixture. Refrigerate at least 30 minutes or until firm enough to shape into balls.

3. Combine coconut, almond flour, sweetened condensed milk and almond extract in small bowl. Set aside.

4. Preheat oven to **400° F.** Set out miniature muffin pans (1¾ x 1-inch). Do not grease.

5. Measure dough in 1 tablespoon portions. With fingers, press dough evenly in bottom and sides of each miniature cup.

6. Bake **14 to 16 minutes** or until golden brown. Remove pan from oven; immediately press candy kiss into each cookie and put 1½-2 teaspoons of coconut mixture on top. Return cookies to oven 3 to 4 minutes, or until filling is set.

7. Cool 6 minutes in pan on wire rack. Use pointed knife to lift cookies out of pan; transfer to wire rack to cool completely. **Frost.**

8. Refrigerate cookies in airtight container up to 3 days or freeze, unfrosted, up to 2 months.

Makes almost 2½ dozen miniature cookie cups

Caramel-Cashew Cookies

Topped with rich caramel frosting, these soft, buttery cookies chock-full of cashews are fabulous. You may want to store some out-of-sight or they may disappear all at once. (Photo page 78)

1½ cups The GF Cookie Lady's Flour (page 4) ¾ teaspoon xanthan gum ¼ teaspoon baking powder ½ teaspoon baking soda ¼ teaspoon freshly grated nutmeg ¼ teaspoon salt
¼ cup (½ stick) unsalted butter ¼ cup solid vegetable shortening 1 cup firmly packed light brown sugar 2 teaspoons pure vanilla extract ½ teaspoon caramel flavoring*
1 large egg ¼ cup sour cream
¾ cup coarsely chopped lightly salted cashews
1 recipe Caramel Frosting (page 143)

Cookie Tip:

 *Caramel flavoring is the secret ingredient that makes these cookies pop. Find it in kitchen specialty stores (Resources page 164).

1. Preheat oven to **350° F**. Line cookie sheets with parchment paper.

2. Sift flour, xanthan gum, baking powder, baking soda, nutmeg and salt in bowl; stir. Set aside.

3. Beat butter, shortening, brown sugar, vanilla and caramel flavoring in large mixer bowl on medium speed until creamy, about 3 minutes. Beat in egg and sour cream. Gradually beat in flour mixture. Stir in nuts.

4. Measure dough in 1½ tablespoon portions; drop 2 inches apart on prepared sheet. Keep dough refrigerated until ready to bake.

5. Bake **14 to 15 minutes** or until golden brown. Cool 3 minutes on cookie sheet then transfer to wire rack to cool completely.

6. **Frost.**

7. Store in airtight container up to 2 days or freeze, unfrosted, up to 2 months.

Makes 2 dozen (2½ inch) cookies

Variation:

 For healthful boost, add ½ cup dried apricots, cut into small pieces.

Naturally Nutty Cookies 83

Coconut Mounds

For coconut enthusiasts: here is a chewy, macaroon-type cookie filled with sweetened coconut, nuts and a whiff of orange.

4 cups sweetened flaked coconut
¼ cup finely chopped pecans
½ cup granulated sugar
3 large egg whites
⅛ teaspoon salt
2 tablespoons unsalted butter, melted
1 teaspoon pure vanilla extract
½ teaspoon pure almond extract
1 teaspoon freshly grated orange zest

1. Preheat oven to **350° F.** Line cookie sheets with parchment paper.

2. Combine all ingredients in large bowl. Use spoon or hands to mix together.

3. Measure mixture by 1½ tablespoon portions; drop 2 inches apart on prepared sheet.

4. Bake **15 minutes** or until edges are lightly browned. Cool 5 minutes on cookie sheet then transfer to wire rack to cool completely.

5. Store in airtight container up to 3 days.

Makes 1½ dozen (1½-inch) cookies

Cookie Tip:

 One 14-oz. package of coconut equals 5⅓ cups.

Variation:

 Drizzle Chocolate Glaze (page 145) over cookies. Dip whisk into chocolate and shake back and forth over cookies for an attractive presentation. If chocolate glaze becomes too thick, dilute with very hot water, a teaspoon at a time, until desired consistency is reached. Garnish with finely chopped pecans.

Lacy Almond Cookies

Crisp and very delicate, these lacy-looking, flourless cookies make for light dessert winners. (Photo page 78)

> ⅓ cup whole raw almonds
> ½ cup granulated sugar
> 2 tablespoons water

1. Preheat oven to **375°F**. Line cookie sheets with non-stick, quick release aluminum foil.

2. Pulverize almonds in bowl of food processor until finely ground, about 30 seconds. Add sugar and water; process until mixture is paste-like about 20 seconds. Let mixture stand 15 minutes.

3. Measure dough in teaspoon portions; drop 4 inches apart on prepared sheet. Dough spreads a lot.

4. Bake **8 to 9 minutes** or until brown and very bubbling. Cool 5 minutes on cookie sheet. Leave cookies on foil and place in freezer 5 more minutes. Remove from freezer and pop cookies off foil. Cookies are very delicate.

5. Store in airtight container up to 3 days or freeze up to 2 months.

Makes 2 dozen (3-inch) cookies

Cookie Tip:

For beautiful presentation, make cut toward top of large strawberry (or chocolate-covered strawberry) and stick cookie inside it. Serve immediately.

Variation:

 For flavor boost, replace granulated sugar with any flavored-scented sugar (Scented Sugars, page 129).

Lemon-Pistachio Cookies

Make a batch of these thin, sweet and chewy on the inside and crisp on the outside cookies. These flourless, nutritional powerhouse cookies are sure to be requested often.

1 cup pistachio butter (page 125)
¾ cup granulated sugar
1 teaspoon pure vanilla extract
1 teaspoon freshly grated lemon zest (1 small lemon)
1 large egg
½ teaspoon baking soda
2 tablespoons confectioners' sugar
⅛ teaspoon ground ginger

Cookie Tips:

 There is more potassium and iron by weight in pistachios than in any other nut, fruit or vegetable. Great little powerhouses!

 These cookies make yummy ice cream cookie sandwiches, especially with pistachio ice cream.

1. Preheat oven to **350° F.** Line cookie sheets with parchment paper.

2. Beat pistachio butter, granulated sugar, vanilla and lemon zest in large mixer bowl on medium speed until mixed, about 1 minute. Beat in egg and baking soda. Let dough stand at room temperature 10 minutes.

3. Measure dough in 1 tablespoon portions; drop 3 inches apart on prepared sheet. Dough is very sticky and spreads a lot.

4. Bake **8 to 9 minutes** or until edges are lightly browned. Cool 3 minutes on cookie sheet then transfer to wire rack to cool completely.

5. Combine confectioners' sugar and ginger in small shaker; sprinkle over cookies.

6. Store in airtight container up to 2 days or freeze up to 2 months.

Makes almost 2 dozen (3-inch) cookies

Mango-Macadamia Cookies

These sweet tropical treasures are chocked filled with macadamias, dried mango, ginger, and bits of coconut.

2½ cups The GF Cookie Lady's Flour (page 4)   1 (3.3 ounce) box <u>instant</u> coconut pudding/pie filling mix   1 teaspoon xanthan gum   1 teaspoon baking soda   ¼ teaspoon salt   1 teaspoon ground ginger
½ cup (1 stick) unsalted butter   ¼ cup canola oil   ⅔ cup firmly packed light brown sugar   2 teaspoons pure vanilla extract
2 large eggs
1 cup coarsely chopped macadamia nuts   1½ cups dried mango, cut into medium-sized pieces and plumb*   ¼ cup sweetened flaked coconut

Cookie Tip:

 *To plumb dried mango: First cut into desired pieces (use kitchen scissors) and cover with very hot water (or other favored liquids). Let stand 5-10 minutes, depending on dryness of fruit. Drain and pat dry with paper towels.

1. Preheat oven to **350° F.** Line cookie sheets with parchment paper.

2. Sift flour, dry pudding mix, xanthan gum, baking soda, salt and ginger in bowl; stir. Set aside.

3. Beat butter, oil, brown sugar and vanilla in large mixer bowl on medium speed until creamy, about 3 minutes. Beat in eggs, one at a time. Gradually beat in flour mixture. Combine nuts, mango and coconut; beat into dough.

4. Measure dough in 1½ tablespoon portions; drop 2 inches apart on prepared sheet. Keep dough refrigerated until ready to bake.

5. Bake **12 to 13 minutes** or until golden brown. Cool 2 minutes on cookie sheet then transfer to wire rack to cool completely. Cookies soften as they sit.

6. Store in airtight container up to 2 days or freeze up to 2 months.

Makes almost 3 dozen (2-inch) cookies

Variations:

 Use freshly grated ginger for a stronger taste (amount depends on taste preference).

 Use combination of dried mango and dried pineapple.

Orange-Glazed Walnut Cookies

Nibble on these moist, cake-like cookies loaded with walnuts and topped with a light orange glaze. (Photo page 78)

1¼ cups The GF Cookie Lady's Flour (page 4)
½ teaspoon xanthan gum
½ teaspoon baking soda
¼ teaspoon baking powder
¼ teaspoon salt
¼ cup (½ stick) unsalted butter
¾ cup firmly packed light brown sugar
½ teaspoon pure vanilla extract
1 large egg
½ cup sour cream
½ cup coarsely chopped walnuts
1 recipe Orange Glaze (page 146)

Cookie Tip:

English walnuts (my favorite) are sold in supermarkets. Black walnuts are darker than English ones and have a more pronounced and buttery flavor. Find black walnuts in high-end specialty food shops.

1. Preheat oven to **375°F**. Line cookie sheets with parchment paper
2. Sift flour, xanthan gum, baking soda, baking powder and salt in bowl; stir. Set aside.
3. Beat butter, brown sugar and vanilla in large mixer bowl on medium speed until creamy, about 4 minutes. Beat in egg and sour cream. Gradually beat in flour mixture. Stir in nuts.
4. Measure dough in 1½ tablespoon portions; drop 2 inches apart on prepared sheet. With lightly moistened hand, flatten dough to ½-inch thickness. Keep dough refrigerated until ready to bake.
5. Bake **13 to 14 minutes** or until cookies puff up and turn light brown. Cool 4 minutes on cookie sheet then transfer to wire rack to cool completely.
6. **Frost.**
7. Store in airtight container up to 2 days or freeze, unfrosted, up to 2 months.

Makes 1½ dozen (2½-inch) cookies

Variations:

Frost with Vanilla Glaze (page 146) and garnish with ⅓ cup finely chopped walnuts.

Replace brown sugar and walnuts with maple-scented sugar (page 130) and maple flavored walnuts (page 128).

Pistachio-Cranberry Cookies

An appealing twosome, crunchy pistachios and tart cranberries, result in cookies worthy of celebrity status.

2 cups The GF Cookie Lady's Flour (page 4)
1 (3.4-oz.) box of <u>instant</u> pistachio pudding/pie filling mix
1 teaspoon xanthan gum
1 teaspoon cream of tartar
1 teaspoon baking soda
¼ teaspoon salt
1 cup (2 sticks) unsalted butter
1½ cups confectioners' sugar
2 teaspoons freshly grated lemon zest (1 lemon)
2 teaspoons pure vanilla extract
2 large eggs
½ cup dried cranberries
⅔ cup coarsely chopped pistachios
1 recipe Lemon Cream Cheese Frosting (page 142)

Cookie Tips:

- Dried cranberries and Craisins® are interchangeable in recipes. Craisins® is the brand name for sweetened dried cranberries.

- Confectioners' sugar and powdered sugar are the same.

1. Preheat oven to **350° F.** Line cookie sheets with parchment paper.

2. Sift flour, dry pudding mix, xanthan gum, cream of tartar, baking soda and salt in bowl; stir. Set aside.

3. Beat butter, confectioners' sugar, lemon zest and vanilla in large mixer bowl on medium speed until creamy, about 4 minutes. Beat in eggs, one at a time. Gradually beat in flour mixture. Stir in cranberries and nuts.

4. Measure dough in 1½ tablespoon portions; drop 3 inches apart on prepared sheet. Keep dough refrigerated until ready to bake.

5. Bake **10 to 11 minutes** or until edges are lightly browned. Cool 3 minutes on cookie sheet then transfer to wire rack to cool completely.

6. **Frost.**

7. Store in airtight container up to 2 days or freeze, unfrosted, up to 2 months.

Makes almost 3 dozen (2½-inch) cookies

Variation:

Garnish frosted cookies with finely chopped pistachios for extra crunch and visual attractiveness.

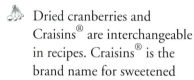

Naturally Nutty Cookies   89

Spicy Maple Nut

Attention all maple lovers: this cookie is for you.
Sweet spices compliment the maple flavor, raisins add chewiness and pecans crunch.

2¼ cups The GF Cookie Lady's GF Flour (page 4)   1½ teaspoons xanthan gum   2 teaspoons baking soda   ½ teaspoon freshly grated nutmeg   1 teaspoon ground cinnamon   1 teaspoon ground ginger   ¼ teaspoon salt
¾ cup solid vegetable shortening   1 cup firmly packed light brown sugar   ½ teaspoon pure maple extract   ½ teaspoon butter flavoring
1 large egg   ¼ cup pure maple syrup
⅓ cup raisins   ½ cup coarsely chopped pecans

Cookie Tips:

- For best results, use 100 % pure maple syrup not artificially-flavored pancake syrup.

- If dough is sticky, refrigerate 30 minutes; then shape into balls.

1. Preheat oven to **375° F.** Line cookie sheets with parchment paper.

2. Sift flour, xanthan gum, baking soda, nutmeg, cinnamon, ginger and salt in bowl; stir. Set aside.

3. Beat shortening, brown sugar, maple extract and butter flavoring in large mixer bowl on medium speed until creamy, about 4 minutes. Beat in egg and maple syrup. Gradually beat in flour mixture. Stir in raisins and pecans.

4. Measure dough in 1½ tablespoon portions; shape into balls and roll in granulated sugar. Drop 3 inches apart on prepared sheet. With lightly moistened hand, flatten balls to ½-inch thickness.

5. Bake **10 to 12 minutes** or until edges are lightly browned. Cool 3 minutes on cookie sheet then transfer to wire rack to cool completely.

6. Store in airtight container up to 2 days or freeze up to 2 months.

Makes 2½ dozen (3-inch) cookies

Variations:

- Roll balls in maple-scented sugar (page 130) and bake as directed.

- Frost cookies with Maple Frosting (page 144).

Walnut-Chocolate Chip Biscotti

My effervescent Italian neighbor, Margie, shared her fabulous biscotti recipe with me. Now made gluten-free, she said they taste just like hers! They are crunchy, not too sweet, and loaded with chocolate chips. (Photo page 78)

1½ cups The GF Cookie Lady's Flour (page 4) ½ teaspoon xanthan gum ½ teaspoon salt
½ cup canola oil ½ cup vanilla-scented sugar (page 131) 1 teaspoon pure vanilla extract 1 teaspoon pure almond extract
2 large eggs
1½ cups whole walnuts ½ cup semisweet chocolate chips

Cookie Tip:

 The secrets in making this biscotti recipe are: beating eggs into fat/sugar mixture 6 minutes; and putting the baked, sliced cookies back into oven (oven turned off) 6-7 hours or overnight.

1. Preheat oven to **350° F.** Line one 15 x 10 x 1-inch jelly roll pan with parchment paper.

2. Sift flour, xanthan gum and salt in bowl; stir. Set aside.

3. Beat oil, vanilla-scented sugar, vanilla and almond extract in large mixer bowl until mixed, about 1 minute. Beat in eggs, one at a time; then beat 6 minutes, scraping sides and bottom of bowl occasionally. Beat in flour mixture. Beat in nuts and chocolate chips.

4. Spread dough into oblong shape (about 12 x 9 x ¼ –inch thickness) with lightly moistened fingers.

5. Bake **20 minutes**. Cool 10 minutes in pan then transfer to cutting board. **Turn oven off.** With serrated knife, cut cookie in half (lengthwise) then slice them on a slight diagonal about 1-inch thick. Arrange cookies on jelly roll pan, cut side up, and return to oven 6-7 hours or overnight. Be sure oven is turned off.

6. Store in airtight container up to 5 days or freeze up to 2 months.

Makes almost 2 dozen (5 x 1-inch) cookies

Variation:

 Dip biscotti in Chocolate Glaze (page 145). For easier dipping, dilute glaze with hot water, a teaspoon at a time, until desired consistency is reached.

No-Bake, No-Fuss Cookies

No fuss, no oven—just quick, easy and delicious! Now that's a delight! You'll have less time preparing and more time enjoying. Some of these are candy-like treats while others are loaded with cereal. My signature bar is the power-packed Grip It & Rip It Granola Bars! If you want a quick treat and fun for kids to make, choose Sweet Pretzel Bites.

- Caramel Nut Clusters 95
- Chocolate Dynabites 96
- Cranberry-Pecan Barkie 97
- Crispy Cappuccino Treats 98
- Crunchy Kiss-A-Roos 99
- Festive Cookie Wreaths 100
- Fudgy Fudge Bars 101
- Grip It & Rip It Granola Bars 102
- Snick-A-Tee Treats 103
- Sweet Nutty Nibbles 104
- White Chocolate-Peanut Crunchers 105

Clockwise from upper left:
Grip It & Rip It Granola Bars (p. 102), Crispy Cappuccino Treats (p. 98), Festive Cookie Wreaths (p. 100), Caramel Nut Clusters (p. 95) and Sweet Nutty Nibbles (p. 104)

No Bake, No Fuss Know-How:

Many of the recipes in this section call for brown rice crisp cereal. Erewhon® Crispy Brown Rice Cereal and Barbara's Brown Rice Crisp cereals are two gluten-free ones. Find both in health related grocery stores and some supermarkets.

Always use fresh moist marshmallows. Hard or gummy marshmallows are tough when melted and produce poor results. Similarly, microwave marshmallows in short intervals, stirring after each interval until melted; or marshmallows may become overcooked and tough.

Toasted nuts are recommended in these recipes because they add extra flavor and crunch. The preferred method for toasting nuts is in the oven (page 122). Since this is a **No Bake** section, you'll find directions in the Cookie Tips for "stovetop toasting." Be sure to watch nuts closely, they burn easily on the stovetop. Note: Stovetop method works best with chopped, as opposed to whole, nuts.

Non-stick aluminum foil, such as Reynolds® Wrap Release®, is the best foil to use when making cereal bars. No cooking spray or cleanup are required, the bars come out neatly and are easier to cut. After bars have set, lift bars from the pan, remove the foil and cut into desired portions.

Use a bench scraper to cut bars. With a bench scraper, you can cut straight down and lift straight out making nice clean cuts. Find this tool in kitchen specialty shops (Photo page 7).

For Best Results:
- Read entire recipe to ensure necessary ingredients and equipment are on hand or if any advance procedure needs to be done.
- Use fresh, crisp cereals; moist soft marshmallows and dried fruit, toasted nuts and other quality ingredients.
- No-bake cookies set up quickly; it's important to prepare pan or cookie sheet as specified in recipe beforehand.
- Measure accurately and mix according to directions.

Caramel Nut Clusters

Is it a cookie or candy? These quick and easy treats make great holiday or hostess gifts. Bet you can't eat just one! (Photo page 92)

25 light-colored caramels, unwrapped
1 tablespoon unsalted butter
1 tablespoon milk

1 (6 oz.) package sliced almonds, toasted (equals 1½ cups)
½ cup coarsely chopped pecans, toasted*
½ cup salted peanuts

1. Line cookie sheet with waxed paper.

2. Put caramels, butter and milk in large microwave-safe bowl. Microwave, uncovered, on High (100 percent power) in 30 second intervals until melted. Stir after each interval. Watch carefully; do not overcook. Remove from microwave; stir in almonds, pecans and peanuts.

3. Drop by small tablespoonfuls on prepared sheet. Mixture is sticky; refrigerate 30 minutes or until set.

4. Store in airtight container in refrigerator up to 3 days.

Makes 2 dozen pieces

Cookie Tip:

 *To stovetop toast nuts: Cook nuts in ungreased skillet over medium-low heat 5 minutes, or until fragrant. Stir often. Cool before using.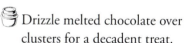

Variations:

Drizzle melted chocolate over clusters for a decadent treat.

Replace with 2½ cups of your favorite nut combination.

Chocolate Dynabites

Quinoa flakes and dried fruits team up to provide a nutritional bite for young and old alike.

2 tablespoons unsalted butter, cut into small pieces
½ cup granulated sugar
2 tablespoons unsweetened cocoa powder
2 tablespoons milk

¼ cup quinoa flakes
¼ cup toffee bits (such as Skor® English Toffee Bits)
¼ cup dried apricots, cut in small pieces
¼ cup raisins
¼ cup dried banana chips, broken into small pieces

1. Line cookie sheet with waxed paper.
2. Put butter, granulated sugar, cocoa powder and milk in large microwave-safe bowl. Microwave, uncovered, on High (100 percent power) in 30 second intervals until melted. Stir after each interval. Remove from microwave. Combine quinoa flakes, toffee bits, apricots, raisins and banana chips; stir into chocolate mixture.
3. Drop by teaspoonfuls on prepared sheet. Refrigerate 30 minutes or until firm.
4. Store in airtight container up to 2 days or freeze up to 2 months.

Makes 2 dozen pieces

Cookie Tips:

- Quinoa flakes, a complete protein grain, provide essential minerals, like calcium and iron to your diet. Find in health-related grocery stores.

- Kitchen scissors cut dried fruits easier than a knife.

Variations:

- Omit candy and banana chips; replace with your favorite nuts.

- Replace quinoa flakes with gluten-free oats.

Cranberry-Pecan Barkie

Variations of this candy-like treat are limited only by your imagination.

---

1 (12-oz.) package vanilla-flavored candy melts (equals 2 cups)
¼ teaspoon ground cinnamon
1½ cups pecans, toasted*
1½ cups dried cranberries

---

1. Line cookie sheet with waxed paper.
2. Put candy melts in large microwave-safe bowl. Microwave, uncovered, on High (100 percent power) in 30 second intervals until melted. Stir after each interval. Remove from microwave; stir in cinnamon. Stir in pecans and dried cranberries.
3. Drop mixture on prepared sheet. Cool 1 hour or until hardened; break into desired pieces.
4. Store in airtight container up to a week.

Makes 24 pieces

Cookie Tips:

 Candy melts and almond bark are interchangeable. Candy melts are preferred; they are creamier. Find in cake decorating aisle at department stores.

 *To stovetop toast pecans: Cook pecans in ungreased skillet over medium-low heat 6 to 8 minutes, or until fragrant. Stir frequently. Cool completely before using.

Variations:

 Replace ground cinnamon, pecans and dried cranberries with ground ginger, toasted walnuts halves and dried chopped apricots.

 Replace white candy melts, pecans and cranberries with light cocoa candy melts, toasted hazelnuts and dried cherries.

Crispy Cappuccino Treats

Here's an adult version to an all time favorite treat with the additions of coffee, chocolate, and nuts. Pour yourself a cappuccino and take a bite of these crispy treats. (Photo page 92)

1 tablespoon boiling water 1 tablespoon <u>instant</u> coffee powder 1 teaspoon pure vanilla extract
4 cups miniature marshmallows
1 cup coarsely chopped pecans, divided ¼ cup butterscotch chips 4 cups brown rice crisp cereal
½ cup chocolate hazelnut spread (such as Nutella®)
¼ cup sweetened flaked coconut

1. Line bottom and sides of 8 x 8 x 2-inch baking pan with non-stick aluminum foil, leave 1 inch overhang.

2. Combine boiling water, instant coffee powder and vanilla in small bowl. Set aside.

3. Put marshmallows in large microwave-safe bowl. Microwave, uncovered, on High (100 percent power) in 30 second intervals until melted. Stir after each interval. Remove from microwave; stir in coffee mixture. Stir in ½ cup nuts, butterscotch chips and cereal.

4. Press mixture firmly in prepared pan. **Frost** with chocolate hazelnut spread. Garnish with remaining nuts (½ cup) and coconut.

5. Refrigerate 1 hour or until firm enough to cut. Remove from pan and cut into bars.

6. Store in airtight container in refrigerator up to 3 days.

Make 16 bars

Cookie Tips:

 Use fresh moist marshmallows. Hard or gummy marshmallows are tough when melted and produce poor results.

 Not all butterscotch chips are gluten-free; check labels.

 Find Nutella® in peanut butter aisle.

Variation:

 Drizzle Chocolate- Mocha Glaze over bars (page 145).

Crunchy Kiss-A-Roos

This crunchy cookie wins on all counts- quick to make, nutritious and delicious. It's topped with a candy kiss for an edge of sweetness.

¼ cup dark corn syrup 2 tablespoons light brown sugar
½ cup creamy peanut butter ½ teaspoon pure vanilla extract
1½ cups Great Granola (page 149)
18 chocolate peanut butter kisses

1. Line cookie sheet with waxed paper.

2. Combine dark corn syrup and brown sugar in large microwave-safe bowl. Microwave, uncovered, on High (100 percent power) 1 minute, stirring after 30 seconds. Remove from microwave; stir in peanut butter and vanilla. Stir in granola.

3. Drop by tablespoonfuls on prepared sheet. Press peanut butter kiss into each cookie.

4. Store in airtight container up to 2 days or freeze up to 2 months.

Makes 18 (1½ -inch) cookies

Cookie Tip:

 Great Granola is very nutritious. Sprinkle it over yogurt or eat by handfuls for a healthy snack.

Variations:

 Omit peanut kiss and replace with your favorite gluten-free candy or whole dried fruit.

 Melt 1 cup chocolate chips with 1 cup butterscotch chips; stir in 2½ cups Great Granola. Drop by tablespoonfuls.

Festive Cookie Wreaths

You'll want to make these for every holiday season. Ho, Ho, Ho! (Photo page 92)

½ cup (1 stick) unsalted butter, cut into chunks 1 (10-oz.) package large marshmallows
1 teaspoon pure vanilla extract ½ teaspoon green food color
4½-5 cups gluten-free cornflakes ¼ cup sweetened flaked coconut
36-40 red M & M® candies

Cookie Tips:

 Find gluten-free cornflakes in health-related food stores.

 Change food color and candies for other seasons. Halloween: use orange food color with black jelly beans. Springtime: use yellow food color with pastel candies.

1. Line cookie sheet with waxed paper.
2. Put butter and marshmallows in large microwave-safe bowl. Microwave, uncovered, on High (100 percent power) in 30 second intervals until melted. Stir after each interval. Remove from microwave; stir in vanilla and food color. Stir in cornflakes and coconut.
3. Drop by tablespoonfuls on prepared sheet. Press one red candy in each cookie.
4. Store in airtight container in refrigerator up to 3 days.

Makes 2½ dozen pieces

Fudgy Fudge Bars

If you want an easy, decadent and very versatile fudge bar, try this one. Use your favorite chocolate, nut flour and filling to suit your taste buds.

2 cups milk chocolate chips (equals 12-oz.)*
½ cup unsalted butter, cut in small pieces
2 cups almond flour**
1 (14-oz.) can sweetened condensed milk
½ teaspoon pure almond extract
1 recipe Cherry Crème Filling (page 137)

1. Line bottom and sides of 8 x 8 x 2-inch pan with non-stick aluminum foil, leave 1-inch overhang.

2. Put chocolate chips and butter in large microwave-safe bowl. Microwave, uncovered, on High (100 percent power) in 30 second intervals until melted. Stir after each interval. Remove from microwave; stir in almond flour, sweetened condensed milk and almond extract. Press mixture evenly in prepared pan. Refrigerate 1 hour or until firm.

3. Make **Cherry Crème Filling.**

4. Cut bars into 25 pieces (5 rows x 5 rows); then cut each piece horizontally to make two equal halves. Spread ½ to 1 teaspoon of filling between pieces; press together to make mini sandwiches.

5. Refrigerate bars in airtight container up to 3 days.

Makes 25 bars

Cookie Tips:

 *Most milk chocolate chips are packaged in 11.5-oz. bag; add 2 tablespoons of chocolate chips to make 12-ounces.

 Chips and chocolate squares are interchangeable: 1 cup of chocolate chips equals 6 (1-oz.) squares.

 **Grind 1⅓ cups whole almonds in food processor until finely ground to make 2 cups of almond flour.

Variations:

 To increase chocolate flavor, replace milk chocolate with 8-oz. semisweet and 4-oz. unsweetened chocolate squares and add 1 teaspoon instant coffee. Cut chocolate squares in small pieces before melting.

 Change fillings (pages 137-140); add spices or dried fruit such as tart cherries.

Grip It & Rip It Granola Bars

Incredibly delicious and surprisingly nutritious, these bars are definitely blue ribbon contenders. (Photo page 92)

4½ -4¾ cups Great Granola (page 149)
½ cup raisins or favorite dried fruit
½ cup granulated sugar
½ cup dark corn syrup
½ cup peanut butter
1 teaspoon pure vanilla extract

Cookie Tip:

 Use bottom of a flat measuring cup (1 cup size) to press mixture firmly into pan.

1. Line bottom and sides of an 11 x 7-inch baking dish with non-stick aluminum foil, leave 1-inch overhang.

2. Combine granola and dried fruit in large bowl. Set aside.

3. Combine granulated sugar and dark corn syrup in microwave-safe bowl. Microwave, uncovered, on High (100 percent power) 1 minute, stirring after 30 seconds. Remove from microwave; stir in peanut butter and vanilla. Pour peanut butter mixture over granola mixture; stir until mixed. (Mixture may not be totally combined but it will stick together as you press it in pan.)

4. Press mixture firmly in prepared pan. Let bars stand 1 to 2 hours or until firm enough to cut. Remove from pan and cut into bars.

5. Individually wrap bars in plastic wrap; then store in resealable plastic bag up to 3 days or freeze up to 2 months.

Makes 14 bars

Variations:

 Substitute ½ cup of pecan butter for peanut butter (page 125).

 Eliminate dried fruit; substitute with more granola.

Snick-A-Tee Treats

You'll snicker when you eat these crunchy treats!
It's hard to resist one of these and even harder to resist a second.

---

3 (2.07-oz.) Snickers®, cut into small pieces
¼ cup unsalted butter, cut into small pieces.
3 tablespoons peanut butter
¾ cup miniature marshmallows

3 cups brown rice crisp cereal
¼ cup coarsely chopped salted peanuts

1 recipe Double Chip Glaze (page 145)

---

1. Line bottom and sides of 8 x 8 x 2- inch baking pan with non-stick aluminum foil, leave 1-inch overhang.

2. Put candy pieces, butter, peanut butter and marshmallows in large microwave-safe bowl. Microwave, uncovered, on High (100 percent power) in 30 second intervals until melted. Stir after each interval. Remove from microwave; stir in cereal and peanuts.

3. Press mixture firmly in prepared pan.

4. **Frost**. Refrigerate bars 30 minutes or until firm enough to cut.

5. Store in airtight container up to 3 days.

Makes 16 bars

Cookie Tip:
Keep marshmallows in freezer for longer shelf life.

Variation:
Frost bars with Peanut Butter Cream Cheese Frosting (page 142).

Sweet Nutty Nibbles

Make these for those times when a small bite of sweetness is all you need and time is a factor. Best if made and eaten right away! (Photo page 92)

Bottom Layer:	1 gluten-free cracker (such as Blue Diamond® Pecan Nut Thin Cracker)
Second Layer:	1 gluten-free round-shaped pretzel
Third Layer:	1 Rolo® candy piece
Fourth Layer:	1 pecan

1. Put cracker on microwave-safe plate. Place pretzel on top of cracker and then put candy on pretzel.

2. Microwave cookie 15-20 seconds. Candy should be soft, not melted. Remove from microwave and immediately press pecan on top.

Makes individual servings

Cookie Tips:

- Blue Diamond® Pecan Nut Thin Crackers and gluten-free pretzels can be found at health-related grocery stores.

- Toast pecans for added crunch and flavor. Keep supply in freezer for convenience (page 122).

Variation:

- Eliminate pretzel layer and use your favorite cracker, candy and nut for an equally tasty and quick snack.

White Chocolate-Peanut Crunchers

These easy, no bake candy-cookies explode with snap, crackle and pop.
You may want to double this recipe.

1 cup (6 oz.) white chocolate chips
¼ cup peanut butter

¾ cup miniature marshmallows
½ cup salted peanuts
½ cup brown rice crisp cereal

1. Line cookie sheet with waxed paper.
2. Put white chocolate chips and peanut butter in large microwave-safe bowl. Microwave, uncovered, on High (100 percent power) in 30 second intervals until melted. Stir after each interval. Combine marshmallows, peanuts and cereal; stir into peanut butter mixture.
3. Drop by spoonfuls on prepared sheet. Refrigerate 1 hour or until set.
4. Refrigerate in airtight container up to 3 days.

Makes almost 2 dozen pieces

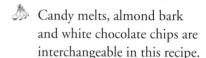

Cookie Tips:

- Candy melts, almond bark and white chocolate chips are interchangeable in this recipe.

- Real white chocolate chips have a very low melting point. If they are allowed to get too hot, they will become grainy; so microwave white chocolate chips in short intervals, stirring until melted.

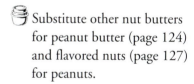

Variations:

- Substitute other nut butters for peanut butter (page 124) and flavored nuts (page 127) for peanuts.

- Substitute semisweet chocolate chips for white chocolate chips; reduce marshmallows by ¼ cup and replace with peanuts or cereal.

106   Peanut Butterlicious Cookies

Peanut Butterlicious Cookies

Peanut butter aficionados told me peanut butter is an American food staple and deserves a separate cookie section. Get ready for a few surprising combinations. Peanut Butter Butterfingers and Peanut Butter Candy Wedges garnered very high marks as did the more challenging Peanut Butter Treasures. Whatever your peanut butter fancy, you'll find it here.

- PB&J Jammers 109
- Peanut Butter-Banana Blasters 110
- Peanut Butter Buns 111
- Peanut Butter Butterfinger'z. 112
- Peanut Butter Candy Wedges 113
- Peanut Butter-Cran Zingers. 114
- Peanut Butter Five-Chippers 115
- Peanut Butter Lollipops 116
- Peanut Butter Monster Cookies 117
- Peanut Butter Treasures 118

Clockwise from upper left:
Peanut Butter-Banana Blasters (p. 110), Peanut Butter Butterfinger'z (p. 112), Peanut Butter Lollipops (p. 116), Peanut Butter Buns (p. 111) and Peanut Butter-Cran Zingers (p. 114)

Peanut Butterlicious Know-How:

Peanuts are really not nuts, but rather legumes that grow and ripen under the ground. Most peanuts are sold roasted—the raw nuts have a softer texture and blander flavor.

Peanut butter is a good source of protein, unsaturated (good) fat, vitamin E, niacin, phosphorous and magnesium.

Peanut butter, by law, must contain a minimum of 90% peanuts with no artificial sweeteners, colors or preservatives. Some brands add about 7% natural sweeteners and 1% salt for taste, plus a stabilizer to keep peanut butter fresh and the oil from separating.

Old-fashioned or natural (organic) peanut butters don't have the stabilizer so the oil separates and needs to be stirred back in before using. Avoid using either one of these peanut butters in my recipes because the consistency is significantly different from the commercial styles of peanut butter and produce inadequate results. Reduced-fat peanut butter will make the cookies drier and a tad tougher. Supermarket brands such as Jif, Skippy, Reese's or Peter Pan are preferable.

Spices that highlight the peanut taste are allspice, ground cinnamon, freshly grated nutmeg, and ground cloves.

Peanut butter flavor can be intensified with chocolate, especially dark chocolate, caramel/butterscotch, brown sugar and vanilla. Peanut butter tastes great with such staples as bananas, apples, celery and raisins to name a few. Try adding some of these staples to your favorite peanut butter cookie recipe.

Using intensified vanilla extract (page 132) and vanilla-scented granulated sugar (page 131) brings out the best flavor in peanut butter.

Before measuring sticky ingredients such as peanut butter or nut butters, spray measuring cup or spoon with vegetable cooking spray. Ingredients won't stick.

For a bold and daring taste, try substituting your favorite nut butter for peanut butter (page 124). For convenience, nut butters may be found in health-related and regular supermarkets.

For Best Results:

- Read entire recipe to ensure necessary ingredients and equipment are on hand or if any advance procedure needs to be done.

- Have **all** ingredients at room temperature. Use quality ingredients.

- Preheat the oven at least 15 minutes. Keep ovenproof thermometer inside oven to ensure accurate temperature.

- Measure accurately and mix according to directions. Scrape bowl often to ensure homogenous dough.

- Use spring-release cookie scoop for uniform size that bakes evenly and at same time.

- Bake one cookie sheet at a time on the middle rack of the oven. Use quality cookie sheets.

- Check cookies at the minimum baking time; continue baking, if necessary, in one-minute intervals. Every oven bakes a little differently. Bake one "test" cookie to gauge baking time in **your** oven. Better to underbake than overbake.

PB&J Jammers

The winning combo of peanut butter and jelly is now made into a cookie.

1½ cups The GF Cookie Lady's Flour (page 4) 1 teaspoon xanthan gum 1 teaspoon baking powder ¼ teaspoon salt
⅓ cup unsalted butter ⅔ cup firmly packed light brown sugar ¼ cup crunchy peanut butter ½ teaspoon pure vanilla extract
1 large egg 2 tablespoons milk
2 tablespoons favorite jam

1. Preheat oven to **350° F**. Line cookie sheets with parchment paper.

2. Sift flour, xanthan gum, baking powder and salt in bowl; stir. Set aside.

3. Beat butter, brown sugar, peanut butter and vanilla in large mixer bowl on medium speed until mixed, about 2 minutes. Beat in egg and milk.

4. Measure dough in 1½ tablespoon portions; drop 2 inches apart on prepared sheet. Press thumb in center of dough to make indentation. Put ¼ teaspoon of jam in indentation.

5. Bake **11 to 12 minutes** or until edges are lightly browned. Cool 2 minutes on cookie sheet then transfer to wire rack to cool completely.

6. Store in airtight container up to 2 days or freeze up to 2 months.

Makes almost 2 dozen (2-inch) cookies.

Cookie Tip:

 Strawberry jam and grape jelly are popular flavors with peanut butter. Other compatible flavors are peach and raspberry jam. Mix and match for everyone's delight.

Variations:

 Sprinkle chopped peanuts over baked cookies.

 Substitute caramel flavoring for vanilla extract.

Peanut Butter-Banana Blasters

When only a crunchy cookie with plenty of banana flavor will do, give this recipe a shot. It's sure to please. (Photo page 106)

1 cup plus 2 tablespoons The GF Cookie Lady's Flour (page 4) ½ (3.4-oz.) box of <u>instant</u> banana crème pudding/pie filling mix ½ teaspoon xanthan gum ½ teaspoon baking soda ⅛ teaspoon salt ¼ teaspoon ground ginger
½ cup (1 stick) unsalted butter ⅓ cup firmly packed light brown sugar ¼ cup granulated sugar ½ teaspoon pure vanilla extract
1 large egg
½ cup peanut butter chips ½ cup salted peanuts ½ cup dried banana chip, broken in small pieces

Cookie Tips:

 ½ (3.4 ounce) box of instant pudding/pie filling mix is equal to ¼ cup. Double the recipe if you like the cookies and use entire box of pudding mix.

1. Preheat oven to **350° F.** Line cookie sheets with parchment paper.

2. Sift flour, dry pudding mix, xanthan gum, baking soda, salt and ginger in bowl; stir. Set aside.

3. Beat butter, brown sugar, granulated sugar and vanilla in large mixer bowl on medium speed until creamy, about 4 minutes. Beat in egg. Gradually beat in flour mixture. Combine peanut butter chips, peanuts and banana chips; beat into dough.

4. Measure dough in 1½ tablespoon portions; roll into balls and drop 2 inches apart on prepared cookie sheets. With slightly moistened hand, flatten dough to ½ -inch thickness. Keep dough refrigerated until ready to bake.

5. Bake **12 to 13 minutes** or until golden brown. Cool 3 minutes on cookie sheet then transfer to wire rack to cool completely.

6. Store in airtight container up to 2 days or freeze, unfrosted, up to 2 months.

Makes almost 2 dozen (2½-inch) cookies

Variations:

Frost cookies with Peanut Butter Cream Cheese Frosting (page 142) or Caramel Frosting (page 143).

Peanut Butter Buns

How divine, decadent peanut butter cookies sandwiched with creamy mousse filling and drizzled with chocolate. Bake a batch and see for yourself. (Photo page 106)

1¼ cups The GF Cookie Lady's Flour (page 4) ¾ teaspoon xanthan gum ½ teaspoon baking soda ⅛ teaspoon salt
½ cup solid vegetable shortening ½ cup firmly packed light brown sugar ½ cup granulated sugar
1 large egg ⅓ cup creamy peanut butter 1 tablespoon hot water
1 recipe Peanut Butter-White Chocolate Mousse Filling (page 139)
1 recipe Chocolate Glaze (page 145)
¼ cup finely chopped peanuts

1. Preheat oven to **375° F.** Line cookie sheets with parchment paper.

2. Sift flour, xanthan gum, baking soda and salt in bowl; stir. Set aside.

3. Beat shortening, brown sugar and granulated sugar in large mixer bowl on medium speed until creamy, about 4 minutes. Beat in egg, peanut butter and hot water. Gradually beat in flour mixture.

4. Measure dough in 1½ tablespoon portions and drop 2 inches apart on prepared cookie sheet.

5. Bake **8 to 10 minutes** or until edges are lightly browned. Watch carefully because cookies brown quickly. Let cookies cool 4 minutes on sheet before transferring to wire rack to cool completely.

6. Make **Peanut Butter-White Chocolate Mousse Filling**. Spread 2 teaspoons of filling on flat side of cookie and place another cookie on top to make cookie sandwiches. **Frost** and garnish with peanuts.

7. Refrigerate cookies in airtight container up to 2 days or freeze, unfrosted, up to 2 months.

Makes 1½ dozen (2½-inch) **cookies**

Cookie Tip:

 Cookies made with solid vegetable shortening are more likely to retain their shape and less likely to spread. Packaged conveniently in sticks and marked in tablespoons and cup measurements, find shortening in baking aisle.

Variations:

 Change flavor of cookie by changing sandwich filling; try Caramel Crème, Chocolate or Oreo® Cream-like Fillings (pages 137-139).

Peanut Butterlicious Cookies 111

Peanut Butter Butterfinger'z

Give this, crisp on the outside and chewy in the middle, cookie a try and be delighted by the peanut butter and butter-finger licking good taste. (Photo page 106)

1 cup The GF Cookie Lady's Flour (page 4)
¼ teaspoon xanthan gum
½ teaspoon baking soda
¼ teaspoon salt
½ cup (1 stick) unsalted butter
¾ cup firmly packed light brown sugar
⅓ cup granulated sugar
½ teaspoon rum extract
½ teaspoon pure almond extract
½ teaspoon pure vanilla extract
1 large egg
1 cup creamy peanut butter
3 (2.1-oz.) coarsely chopped Butterfinger® candy bars (about 1¼ cups)

Cookie Tip:

 These cookies make great ice cream cookie sandwiches, especially with chocolate, caramel or vanilla ice cream.

1. Preheat oven to **350° F.** Line cookie sheets with parchment paper.

2. Sift flour, xanthan gum, baking soda and salt in bowl; stir. Set aside.

3. Beat butter, brown sugar, granulated sugar, rum, almond and vanilla extracts in large mixer bowl on medium speed until creamy, about 4 minutes. Beat in egg and peanut butter. Gradually beat in flour mixture. Beat in candy.

4. Measure dough in 2 tablespoon portions; drop 3 inches apart on prepared sheet. With your hand, slightly flatten dough to ½-inch thickness. Keep dough refrigerated until ready to bake.

5. Bake **13 to 15 minutes** or until edges are lightly browned. Cookies puff in oven and deflate when cooled. Cool 5 minutes on cookie sheet then transfer to wire rack to cool completely.

6. Store in airtight containers up to 2 days or freeze up to 2 months.

Makes 2 dozen (3-inch) cookies

Variation:

 Reduce candy pieces to 1 cup and add ¼ cup raisins for nutritional boost.

Peanut Butter Candy Wedges

What could be more fun than finding candy wedged inside of cookies? Got milk?

1¾ cups The GF Cookie Lady's Flour (page 4)
½ teaspoon xanthan gum
½ teaspoon baking soda
½ teaspoon baking powder
¼ teaspoon salt
½ cup (1 stick) unsalted butter
½ cup firmly packed light brown sugar
½ cup granulated sugar
1 teaspoon pure vanilla extract
1 large egg
½ cup creamy peanut butter
2 (2.07 oz) Snickers® candy bars, cut each bar in 12 pieces; freeze

Cookie Tips:

 If dough is too sticky to form into balls, refrigerate 30 minutes.

 Freezing candy pieces before placing them inside dough minimizes candy oozing out of the cookie as it bakes.

Variation:

 Replace Snickers® with your favorite gluten-free candy.

1. Preheat oven to **375 °F.** Line cookie sheets with parchment paper

2. Sift flour, xanthan gum, baking soda, baking powder and salt in bowl; stir. Set aside.

3. Beat butter, brown sugar, granulated sugar and vanilla in large mixer bowl on medium speed until creamy, about 4 minutes. Beat in egg and peanut butter. Gradually beat in flour mixture.

4. Wrap 1½ tablespoons of dough around each frozen candy piece and roll into balls. Make sure candy is completely covered by dough. Roll balls into granulated sugar and place 3 inches apart on prepared sheet. Keep dough refrigerated until ready to bake.

5. Bake **10 to 11 minutes** or until edges are lightly browned. Cool 4 minutes on cookie sheet then transfer to wire rack to cool completely.

6. Store in airtight container up to 2 days or freeze up to 2 months.

Makes 2 dozen (3-inch) cookies

Peanut Butter-Cran Zingers

The unusual combination of peanut butter, dried cranberries and white chocolate chips blend together, to make this cookie a mouth-watering favorite—a real zinger. (Photo page 106)

1¼ cups The GF Cookie Lady's Flour (page 4)
½ teaspoon xanthan gum
¾ teaspoon baking soda
½ teaspoon baking powder
¼ teaspoon salt
¼ cup (½ stick) unsalted butter
¼ cup solid vegetable shortening
½ cup firmly packed light brown sugar
½ cup granulated sugar
½ teaspoon pure vanilla extract
1 large egg
½ cup creamy peanut butter
¼ cup dried cranberries
¼ cup white chocolate chips
¼ cup salted chopped peanuts

Cookie Tips:

- For best flavor, buy white chocolate chips that list cocoa butter as second ingredient.

- Using combination of butter and vegetable shortening provides cookies with good flavor and less spread.

1. Preheat oven to **375° F.** Line cookie sheets with parchment paper.

2. Sift flour, xanthan gum, baking soda, baking powder and salt in bowl; stir. Set aside.

3. Beat butter, shortening, brown sugar, granulated sugar and vanilla in large mixer bowl on medium speed until creamy, about 4 minutes. Beat in egg and peanut butter. Gradually beat in flour mixture. Combine cranberries, white chocolate chips and peanuts; beat into dough.

4. Measure dough in 2 tablespoon portions; drop 3 inches apart on prepared sheet. With hand, slightly flatten dough to ½-inch thickness.

5. Bake **11 to 13 minutes** or until edges are lightly browned. Cool 5 minutes on cookie sheet then transfer to wire rack to cool completely.

6. Store in airtight container up to 2 days or freeze up to 2 months.

Makes almost 2 dozen (3-inch) cookies

Variation:

Drizzle Chocolate Glaze over cookies (page 145).

Peanut Butterlicious Cookies

Peanut Butter Five-Chippers

Tasters gave a high-five when scoring this chewy cookie packed with five different flavored morsels, nutritious quinoa flakes and crunchy peanut butter.

1 cup The GF Cookie Lady's Flour (page 4) ½ teaspoon xanthan gum 1 teaspoon baking soda ¼ teaspoon salt
½ cup (1 stick) unsalted butter ⅓ cup firmly packed light brown sugar ½ cup granulated sugar 1 teaspoon pure vanilla extract
1 large egg ½ cup crunchy peanut butter
½ cup quinoa flakes ⅓ cup milk chocolate chips ⅓ cup butterscotch chips ⅓ cup white chocolate chips ⅓ cup semisweet chocolate chips ⅓ cup peanut butter chips

Cookie Tips:

- Quinoa flakes, a complete protein, is high in calcium, phosphorous and iron. Find in health related grocery stores.

- Not all butterscotch chips are gluten-free, read labels.

Variation:

Replace quinoa flakes with gluten-free oats (Resources page 163).

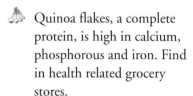

1. Preheat oven to **350° F.** Line cookie sheets with parchment paper.

2. Sift flour, xanthan gum, baking soda and salt in bowl; stir. Set aside.

3. Beat butter, brown sugar, granulated sugar and vanilla in large mixer bowl on medium speed until creamy, about 4 minutes. Beat in egg and peanut butter. Gradually beat in flour mixture. Combine quinoa flakes and all flavored chips; beat into dough.

4. Measure dough in 1½ tablespoon portions; drop 3 inches apart on prepared sheets.

5. Bake **11 to 13 minutes** or until edges are lightly browned. Cool 3 minutes on cookie sheet then transfer to wire rack to cool completely.

6. Store in airtight container up to 2 days or freeze up to 2 months.

Makes 2½ dozen (2½ -inch) cookies

Peanut Butter Lollipops

As you bite into this giant peanut butter cookie on a stick, you'll be delighted to uncover the candy bar surprise tucked inside. (Photo page 106)

1¾ cups The GF Cookie Lady's Flour (page 4)
½ teaspoon xanthan gum
½ teaspoon baking soda
½ teaspoon baking powder
¼ teaspoon salt
½ cup (1 stick) unsalted butter
½ cup firmly packed light brown sugar
½ cup granulated sugar
1 teaspoon pure vanilla extract
1 large egg
½ cup creamy peanut butter
10 (.65-oz.) Baby Ruth® candy bars
10 (4½ x ¼-inch) wooden ice cream sticks

1. Preheat oven to **375 °F.** Line cookie sheets with parchment paper.

2. Gently insert wooden stick ¾ of the way into each candy bar. Place inside freezer until ready to use.

3. Sift flour, xanthan gum, baking soda, baking powder and salt in bowl; stir. Set aside.

4. Beat butter, brown sugar, granulated sugar and vanilla in large mixer bowl on medium speed until creamy, about 4 minutes. Beat in egg and peanut butter. Gradually beat in flour mixture.

5. Wrap ¼ cup of dough around each prepared candy bar. Be sure dough covers candy bar completely. Reshape uneven edges of dough with hands for a more uniform appearance. Place 4 inches apart on prepared sheets. Cookies spread! Keep dough refrigerated until ready to bake.

6. Bake **14 to 16 minutes** or until edges are lightly browned. Cool 6 minutes on cookie sheet then carefully transfer to wire rack to cool completely.

7. Store in airtight container up to 2 days or freeze up to 2 months.

Makes 10 (4-inch) cookies on a stick

Cookie Tips:

 Nestlé® makes a 10 pack Baby Ruth® package. Each bar measures about 2 inches. One package makes one cookie recipe. If unavailable, buy large candy bars and cut to size.

 Wrap giant cookies in cellophane tied in ribbon or purchase decorated bags and give as gifts with the message: "Your heart is as big as this cookie. Thanks for being my friend."

Variation:

 Snickers® bars cut into 2 inch pieces may be substituted.

Peanut Butter Monster Cookies

This flourless cookie packed with peanut butter, gluten-free oats, candy pieces and sunflower seeds make this cookie monstrously good.

2¼ cups gluten-free oats*   ¼ teaspoon salt   1 teaspoon baking soda
¼ cup unsalted butter   ½ cup firmly packed light brown sugar   ½ cup granulated sugar   1 teaspoon pure vanilla extract
2 large eggs   ⅔ cup peanut butter   1 teaspoon corn syrup
½ cup chocolate chips   ½ cup M&M® candies   ¼ cup shelled sunflower seeds

Cookie Tip:

 *Find suppliers for gluten-free oats in Resources (page 163).

1. Combine oats, salt and baking soda in bowl; stir. Set aside.

2. Beat butter, brown sugar, granulated sugar and vanilla in large mixer bowl on medium speed until mixed, about 1½ minutes. Beat in eggs, one at a time, peanut butter and corn syrup. Beat in oat mixture. Combine chocolate chips, candies and sunflower seeds; beat into dough.

3. Cover and refrigerate dough 1 hour or until firm enough to form into balls.

4. Preheat oven to **350° F.** Line cookie sheets with parchment paper.

5. Measure dough in 1½ tablespoon portions; roll into balls and flatten each into ½-inch thickness.

6. Bake **11 to 12 minutes** or until edges are lightly browned. Cool 3 minutes on cookie sheet then transfer to wire rack to cool completely.

7. Store in airtight container up to 2 days or freeze up to 2 months.

Makes almost 2½ dozen (3-inch) cookies

Variations:

If gluten-free oats are not in your diet, use quinoa flakes. Find at health related grocery stores.

Omit sunflower seeds and replace with chopped peanuts.

Peanut Butter Treasures

Tasters agree: This bite-size cookie is cute as a button and tasty as ever with its peanut butter flavor and caramel filling.

½ cup The GF Cookie Lady's Flour (page 4)
⅛ teaspoon xanthan gum
¼ teaspoon baking soda
⅛ teaspoon baking powder
⅛ teaspoon salt
¼ cup (½ stick) unsalted butter
¼ cup firmly packed light brown sugar
¼ cup granulated sugar
½ teaspoon pure vanilla extract
1 large egg
¾ cup peanut butter
1 recipe Caramel Crème Filling (page 137)

1. Preheat oven to **350° F.** Spray miniature muffin pans (1¾ x 1-inch) with vegetable cooking spray.

2. Sift flour, xanthan gum, baking soda, baking powder and salt in bowl; stir. Set aside.

3. Beat butter, brown sugar, granulated sugar and vanilla in large mixer bowl on medium speed until creamy, about 4 minutes. Beat in egg and peanut butter. Gradually beat in flour mixture.

4. Measure dough in 2 teaspoon portions; drop into prepared muffin cups. Press dough slightly into cups.

5. Bake **13 to 14 minutes** or until golden brown. Remove pan from oven; immediately make small indentation in center of each cookie with the back side of ¼ teaspoon spoon, (about ¼-inch down). Cookie will crack a little as utensil is press into it. Cool 10 minutes in pan. Use tip of pointed toothpick to lift cookies out of pan; transfer to cooling rack to cool completely.

6. Make **Caramel Crème Filling**. Put ½ teaspoon of filling in each cookie cup.

7. Store in airtight container up to 2 days or freeze up to 2 months.

Makes almost 3 dozen cookies

Cookie Tips:

 Measure dough portions easier and more accurately with a 2 teaspoon measuring spoon; find it in kitchen specialty shops. It comes in a set of three along with a 2 tablespoon and 1½ tablespoon.

 If filling gets sticky, microwave 10 seconds to improve consistency.

Variations:

 Make ½ recipe of Double Chip Glaze (page 145); drizzle each cookie with ¼ teaspoon. Garnish with finely chopped peanuts.

 Replace Caramel Crème Filling with Chocolate Filling (page 137).

Beyond Cookies

In this section you'll find ways to embellish gluten-free cookies.

All About Nuts 121
   How to Toast Nuts 122
   How to Skin Nuts 123
   How to Make Nut Flours 123
   How to Make Nut Butters 124
   How to Make Almond Paste 126
   How to Make Flavored Nuts 127

Flavored Scented Sugars & More 129

Sweet Fillings 133
   Variations for Fruity-Filled Pinwheels 134
   Sandwich and Layer Fillings 137

Fantastic Frostings & Glazes 141

Your Favorite Recipes:

All About Nuts

Nuts provide extra flavor, texture and nutritional value to gluten-free cookies. Here, you'll learn how to toast nuts, remove skins and make nut flours. Five nut butter recipes, three ways to make almond paste and five delicious flavored-nut recipes will help you embellish cookies and make your family and friends beg for more.

For a sweet and extra crunchy addition to your baked goods and salads, substitute flavored nuts for the unsweetened varieties. Make large batches of flavored nuts and freeze them for baking convenience or gift-giving opportunities. Put nuts in a cellophane bag, wrap with ribbon and write a note, such as "I'm nuts over you", "I'd go nuts without your help", "In this nutty world, you make life fun."

How to Toast Nuts

Nuts are best when lightly toasted. Toasting the nuts releases their natural oils, heightens flavor and increases their crunchiness. To save time, toast a large batch and store in the freezer for future use. Follow these easy steps for toasting nuts to perfection:

- Preheat oven to **325°F.**

- Spread same variety of nuts in a single layer on an ungreased baking pan to promote even baking. Nuts vary in size, oil content and require different baking times.

- Follow the baking times listed below for best result.

- Use fragrance and touch as a guide to determine optimal toasting. Nuts should smell very fragrant and feel warm or hot.

- **Watch closely**; nuts burn easily because of their high oil content. Burnt or overly roasted nuts are bitter and must be discarded.

- Cool nuts completely before storing. If not, the residual heat in the nuts will create moisture in the storage container and soften them.

- Freeze nuts in an airtight plastic bag or plastic or glass container up to 1 year.

Nuts	Temperature	Time
Almonds	325° F.	10 to 11 minutes
Hazelnuts (filberts)	325° F.	6 to 7 minutes
Macadamias	325° F.	7 to 8 minutes
Pecans	325° F.	8 to 10 minutes
Pine Nuts	325° F.	3 to 4 minutes
Pistachios	325° F.	6 to 8 minutes
Walnuts	325° F.	10 to 12 minutes

Cashews are not listed because most are sold roasted.

Stovetop Toasting:

If you're in a hurry and need to toast a few nuts, especially small nuts like pine nuts and sliced or slivered almonds, stovetop toasting is satisfactory. However, more attention is required. **For stovetop toasting:** cook nuts in a heavy skillet over medium-low heat until nuts are fragrant, lightly colored and warm or hot to the touch. Shake the skillet and stir frequently to prevent nuts from burning. While this method works when you are in a hurry, nothing matches the flavor or even browning of oven toasted nuts.

How to Skin Nuts

Some recipes call for the skin to be removed from nuts like hazelnuts (filberts) and almonds. The skin on hazelnuts is very bitter and its best if removed before using them in baked goods. Almond skin is not bitter; but is removed when a colorless, fine and smooth texture is wanted as in making almond paste or marzipan. Otherwise, it's best to keep skin on almonds to increase fiber in the baked goods.

Here's how to skin nuts:

For Hazelnuts: Spread shelled hazelnuts in ungreased baking pan; bake in preheated **325°F** oven **10 to 15 minutes**, or until skins begin to flake. Stir occasionally. Remove from oven and put a handful at a time in a clean, dry cotton kitchen towel; rub vigorously until most of the skins come off. **Note**: Don't worry if some of the skins remain on the nuts. You can't remove all of the skins and toasting has made the skins less bitter.

For Almonds: Blanch whole raw almonds in pan of rapidly boiling water 1 to 2 minutes, or until skin loosens when tested. Pour nuts in colander to drain. Put a handful at a time in a clean, dry cotton kitchen towel; rub briskly until skins come off. If necessary, use your fingers to pinch skin off. **Note**: Blanch means to immerse food briefly in boiling water to help loosen or remove skins or to precook briefly to set color and flavor.

How to Make Nut Flours

Almonds, hazelnuts, chestnuts and other nuts make good nut flours and add a nutritional boost to cookies. **The GF Cookie Lady's Flour** includes almond flour for that very reason. I make my own almond flour by pulverizing whole nuts in the food processor until finely ground. That's it. It is easy to do and very economical.

Some nuts benefit by adding a little sugar to them while processing. Sugar prevents nuts from turning paste-like.

For convenience, nut flours may be purchased in natural/ health food stores, specialty grocery stores such as Trader's Joe or Whole Foods or online (Resources page 162). Commercially refined nut flours (either blanched or with skins on) have a finer texture and may be preferred. Nut flours are highly perishable because of the oil content and should be stored either in the refrigerator or freezer.

How to Make Nut Butters

Most nut butters can be commercially purchased for convenience. If you have a food processor, nut butters are easy to make. When a recipe calls for peanut butter, substitute different nut butters for a wonderful variety of flavors. If you want to experiment and make your own, here are a few of my favorite nut butter sensations.

Almond Butter

Makes ½ cup

1 cup whole raw almonds
¼ teaspoon salt
2 tablespoons honey
2 tablespoons canola oil

Pulverize almonds in food processor until finely ground, about 1½ minutes. Add remaining ingredients; process until paste-like, about 1 minute. Stop food processor occasionally to scrape sides. Store in airtight container in refrigerator up to 2 weeks. Use at room temperature.

Cinnamon-Almond Butter

Makes ¾ cup

¾ cup whole raw almonds
3 tablespoons unsalted butter
3 tablespoons granulated sugar
¼ teaspoon salt
1 teaspoon ground cinnamon

Pulverize almonds in food processor until finely ground, about 1½ minutes. Add remaining ingredients; process until paste-like, about 1 minute. Stop food processor occasionally to scrape sides. Store in airtight container in refrigerator up to 2 weeks. Use at room temperature.

Cashew-Almond Butter

Makes ¾ cup

1 cup lightly salted cashews
1 cup whole raw almonds
3 tablespoons light brown sugar
2 tablespoons canola oil
¼ teaspoon salt

Pulverize nuts in food processor until finely ground, about 1½ minutes. Add remaining ingredients; process until paste-like, about 1 minute. Stop food processor occasionally to scrape sides. Store in airtight container in refrigerator up to 2 weeks. Use at room temperature.

Pecan Butter

Makes ¾ cup

1½ cups pecans, toasted*
¼ teaspoon salt
1½ tablespoons pure maple syrup
1 teaspoon canola oil

Pulverize nuts in food processor until finely ground, about 1½ minutes. Add remaining ingredients; process until paste-like, about 1 minute. Stop food processor occasionally to scrape sides. Store in airtight container in refrigerator up to 2 weeks. Use at room temperature.

***To toast pecans:** Spread pecans in ungreased baking pan. Bake in preheated 325°F oven **8 to 10 minutes**, or until fragrant; cool completely.

Pistachio Butter

Makes 1⅛ cups

1 cup raw pistachios
¼ cup whole dried apricots
⅓ cup confectioners' sugar
3 tablespoons canola oil
½ teaspoon freshly grated lemon zest
¼ teaspoon lemon extract

Pulverize nuts and apricots in food processor until finely ground, about 1½ minutes. Add remaining ingredients; process until paste-like, about 1 minute. Stop food processor occasionally to scrape sides. Keep in airtight container in refrigerator up to 2 weeks. Use at room temperature.

How to Make Almond Paste

Store bought almond paste is made from finely ground blanched almonds, sugar and water and sometimes glucose or egg white. It is not to be confused with marzipan, a similar confection with a higher ratio of sugar to almonds. Not all brands of almond paste are gluten-free. Glucose in some brands is derived from wheat. Call companies to verify.

If you can't find almond paste, here is a simple recipe to make. All you need is a food processor. The Apricot Almond Bars (page 27) has almond paste as an ingredient.

Almond Paste

Makes 1 cup

Can use this almond paste for Apricot Almond Bars, (page 27)

1¼ cup raw whole almonds, blanched*
1 cup confectioners' sugar
1 large pasteurized egg white, slightly beaten
½ teaspoon pure vanilla extract

Pulverize blanched almonds in food processor until finely ground, about 1 minute. Turn processor off; add confectioners' sugar and process until incorporated. Add egg white and almond extract; process until mixture makes ball, scraping sides and bottom of bowl occasionally. Divide paste into 4 (¼ cup portions), individually wrap in plastic wrap; store in resealable plastic bag in freezer up to 2 months. Use at room temperature.

Note: *Blanched means the skins are removed from almonds (page 123).

Tip:

 Find pasteurized egg whites in a pourable carton in refrigerated dairy section.

Variations:

 To make **Cherry Almond Paste**: add 1-2 teaspoons cherry extract and 1 drop of red food color.

 To make **Orange Almond Paste**: add 1-2 tablespoons of freshly grated orange zest, ¼ teaspoon orange oil or extract and 1 drop of orange food color.

How to Make Flavored Nuts

When a recipe calls for nuts, try flavored nuts for extraordinary taste. Besides giving cookies the "wow" factor, they are great as snacks, on top of salads and make unique healthy gifts. As a general rule, pecans and walnuts can be interchanged as can almonds and hazelnuts (filberts).

Our favorites are Cinnamon Almonds and Citrus Nuts. Cinnamon Almonds taste like the ones sold at fairs and festivals and Citrus Nuts are simply divine and addictive!

Cinnamon Almonds

Makes 4 cups

1 cup granulated sugar
⅓ cup water
1 tablespoon ground cinnamon
½ teaspoon salt
2 teaspoons pure vanilla extract
4 cups whole raw almonds

Combine sugar, water, cinnamon and salt in 2-quart saucepan. Bring to a boil; cook 2 minutes over medium heat, stirring occasionally. Remove from heat; stir in vanilla and almonds until well coated. Transfer nuts to aluminum foil to cool completely. Use fork to separate clusters. Store in resealable plastic bag up to 2 weeks or freeze.

Citrus Nuts

Makes 3 cups

1 large egg white
1½ cups whole raw almonds
1½ cups pecans
1 cup confectioners' sugar
¼–½ teaspoon ground cinnamon (to taste)
2 teaspoons freshly grated orange zest (1 small orange)
1 teaspoon freshly grated lemon zest
2 tablespoons freshly squeezed lemon juice (1 medium lemon)

Preheat oven to **300°F**. Spray 18 x 12 x 1-inch pan with vegetable cooking spray. Beat egg white with electric mixer until soft peaks form. Add almonds and pecans; stir until coated. Stir in confectioners' sugar, cinnamon, orange and lemon zest and lemon juice. Spread nuts in single layer in prepared pan. Bake **30 minutes**, stirring after 15 minutes. Turn off oven; keep nuts in oven for another 15 minutes. Transfer nuts to aluminum foil to cool completely. Store in resealable plastic bag up to 2 weeks or freeze.

Maple Nuts

Makes 2 cups

⅓ cup pure maple syrup
1-2 teaspoons freshly grated orange zest, (1 small orange)
2 cups walnuts, toasted*

Heat syrup and orange zest to boiling in small saucepan; stir constantly. Reduce heat to low; stir in walnuts until well coated. Transfer nuts to aluminum foil to cool completely. Store in resealable plastic bag up to 2 weeks or freeze.

***To toast walnuts:** Spread walnuts in ungreased baking pan; bake in preheated **325°F. 10 to 12 minutes**, or until fragrant. Cool completely.

Praline Pecans

Makes 3½ cups

3½ cups pecans
¼ cup dark corn syrup
¼ cup firmly packed light brown sugar
2 tablespoons unsalted butter
¼ teaspoon salt
1 teaspoon pure vanilla extract
¼ teaspoon baking soda

Preheat oven to **250°F.** Spray 18 x 12 x 1-inch pan with vegetable cooking spray. Put pecans in large bowl; set aside. Combine corn syrup, brown sugar, butter and salt in microwave-safe bowl; microwave, uncovered, on High (100 percent power) 1 to 1½ minutes, or until mixture boils. Stir frequently. Remove from microwave; stir in vanilla and baking soda. Pour mixture over pecans; stir until well coated. Spread nuts in single layer on prepared pan. Bake **1 hour**, stirring every 15 minutes. Transfer nuts to aluminum foil to cool completely. Break clusters apart with fork or hands. Store in resealable plastic bag up to 2 weeks or freeze.

Sweet and Spicy Nuts

Makes 4 cups

2 tablespoons unsalted butter, melted
2 tablespoons light corn syrup
2 teaspoons granulated sugar
1 teaspoon ground cinnamon
¼ teaspoon freshly grated nutmeg
¼ teaspoon salt
4 cups favorite raw nut (about 1 pound)

Preheat oven to **250°F.** Combine melted butter, corn syrup, sugar, cinnamon, nutmeg and salt in bowl. Add nuts, stirring until well coated. Spread nuts in single layer on ungreased 18 x 12 x 1-inch pan . Bake **1 hour**, stirring every 15 minutes. Transfer nuts to aluminum foil to cool completely. Store in resealable plastic bag up to 2 weeks or freeze.

Flavored Scented Sugars & More

Want to make your gluten-free cookies even more delicious and receive rave reviews? Make scented sugars and intensified vanilla extract, and purchase vanilla powder. They add great flavor and pizzazz to frostings, fillings and cookies.

Scented sugars can be used in any recipe calling for granulated sugar or can be sprinkled on cookies or in beverages for extra flavor. They can be made with edible flowers, herbs and spices, citrus zest, maple chunks or from vanilla beans. Experiment with the quantity of aromatic material, adding more gradually to increase the sugar's aromatic power. Make in small or large quantities and store conveniently in airtight containers.

Vanilla-scented sugar is my all-time favorite and is an essential ingredient in my pantry.

Citrus-Scented Sugar (Lemon, Lime or Orange)

Makes about 2 cups

3-4 tablespoons freshly grated citrus zest (4 large lemons or 4 large limes or 3 large oranges)
2 cups granulated sugar

Preheat oven to **200°F**. Combine favorite citrus zest and sugar; spread mixture evenly on ungreased baking pan. Bake **15 minutes**, stirring after 7 minutes (sugar is chunky and somewhat hard). Cool 10 minutes in pan. Transfer mixture to bowl of food processor; process until finely ground, about 30 seconds. Keep scented-sugar in airtight container at room temperature up to 2 months. Sugar may clump up over time and should be strained through a sieve before using.

Tips:

 Use a Microplane® Grater, found in kitchen specialty shops, to remove zest only. The white pith from citrus fruit has a bitter flavor and should not be grated.

 For a quicker method, place freshly grated citrus zest and sugar in bowl of food processor; process 30 seconds or until blended. Keep in airtight container in the refrigerator up to 3 weeks.

Variations:

 Flower-Scented Sugar: Replace citrus zest with a handful of dried edible flowers such as calendula.

 Herb-Scented Sugar: Replace citrus zest with 1-2 tablespoons dried herbs such as mint leaves, thyme, rosemary or lavender.

Maple-Scented Sugar

Makes 1¼ cup

1 cup granulated sugar   1 teaspoon maple extract

Put ingredients in bowl of food processor; process until blended, about 30 seconds. Store in airtight container at room temperature up to 2 months.

Spice-Scented Sugar

Makes 1 cup

1 cup granulated sugar
1 teaspoon ground cinnamon
½ teaspoon freshly grated nutmeg
¼ teaspoon ground ginger
⅛ teaspoon ground cloves

Put ingredients in jar. Screw lid on; shake until mixed. Store jar at room temperature up to 2 months.

Vanilla-Scented Confectioners' Sugar

Makes 1 cup

1 cup confectioners' sugar
½ teaspoon vanilla powder*

Put ingredients in jar. Screw lid on; shake until mixed. Store in jar at room temperature up to 2 months.

Tips:

  *Find vanilla powder in specialty or health related stores. I use Authentic Foods™ vanilla powder. (Resource page 162)

  For recipes calling for confectioners' sugar, replace with vanilla-scented confectioners' sugar for a flavor jolt.

Vanilla-Scented Sugar

3 (6-7-inch) moist vanilla beans   5 pounds granulated sugar

Use sharp paring knife to split each vanilla bean down the center to expose tiny seeds. Put one-third of the sugar in large storage container and one split vanilla bean. Layer the remaining sugar and beans. Cover container tightly and store in pantry. After 2 days, gently mix sugar with spoon, or shake container, to shift the vanilla beans. Repeat process in 2 days. After 4 days, sugar is ready to be used. Store up to one year.

Tips:

  If sugar clumps during storage, strain through sieve before using.

Intensified Vanilla Extract

1 (any size) bottle 100 % pure vanilla extract
1 (6-7 inch) whole vanilla bean

Split vanilla bean down the center using a small sharp knife to expose the tiny seeds. Place bean in bottle of pure vanilla extract. When extract is finished, don't discard the aged vanilla bean. Let it dry out and put it and sugar into the bowl of a food processor; process until finely ground. Voila… vanilla-scented sugar!

Tips:

 Find reasonably priced pure vanilla extract, such as Madagascar, in wholesale membership stores.

 Find economical and quality vanilla beans at Penzeys Spices (Resources page 164).

Sweet Fillings

Fillings give cookies a flavor boost and add visual appeal. Some fillings provide a nutritional benefit, while others add extra sweetness to bolster the taste. The pinwheel fillings, made with fruits and nuts, provide a healthy bonus; while creamy sandwich and layer fillings satisfy your sweet tooth. Try different fillings for the same cookie dough and taste the difference!

Master one dough—Fruity-Filled Pinwheels recipe (page 70)—and produce a variety of cookie flavors appealing to everyone's taste buds by simply changing the filling. My taste testers loved the Apple-Raisin, Apricot-Coconut and Raspberry-Apricot. Have fun experimenting to find your favorite.

Use the sandwich and layer fillings recipes to sweeten up your favorite cookies and brownies.

Peanut Butter Buns, recipe found on page 111.

Variations for Fruity-Filled Pinwheels

For best results and ease of preparation, five filling recipes direct you to use a food processor. If necessary, an alternative method is to finely chop nuts and finely cut up fruit by hand. A longer cooking time may be required for the fruit and nut mixture to achieve desired consistency.

Apple-Raisin Filling

Makes 1 cup

¾ cup raisins
½ cup water
¼ cup granulated sugar
½ cup walnuts
¼ teaspoon freshly grated nutmeg
1 tablespoon apple jelly

Put ingredients in bowl of food processor; process until finely ground and paste-like, about 30 seconds. Transfer mixture to small saucepan; cook over medium heat 5 to 6 minutes, or until mixture is reduced to thick paste. Stir often. Cool.

Apricot-Coconut Filling

Makes 1 cup

¾ cup apricot preserves
¼ cup sweetened flaked coconut
½ teaspoon pure almond extract
¼ teaspoon ground ginger
2-3 tablespoons finely chopped walnuts (optional)

Combine ingredients in bowl. If needed, microwave filling 10 to 15 seconds to improve spreading consistency.

Cherry-Almond Filling

Makes 1 cup

½ cup dried cherries
½ cup whole raw almonds
¼ cup apple juice
¼ cup granulated sugar
1 teaspoon pure almond extract

Put ingredients (except almond extract) in bowl of food processor; process until finely ground and paste-like, about 30 seconds. Transfer mixture to a small saucepan; cook over medium heat 5 to 6 minutes, or until mixture is reduced to thick paste. Stir often. Stir in almond extract. Cool.

Cherry-Raisin Filling

Makes 1 cup

¼ cup dried tart cherries
½ cup raisins
½ cup water
¼ cup cherry preserves
¼ teaspoon ground cinnamon
Pinch of ground cloves

Put ingredients in bowl of food processor; process until finely ground and paste-like, about 30 seconds. Transfer mixture to small saucepan; cook over medium heat 7 to 8 minutes, or until mixture is reduced to thick paste. Stir often. Cool.

Date-Pecan Filling

Makes ⅔ cup

2 tablespoons light brown sugar
1 teaspoon cornstarch
½ cup packed whole pitted dates
½ cup sour cream
½ teaspoon pure vanilla extract
1 large egg yolk
⅓ cup pecans

Combine dates, brown sugar and cornstarch in bowl of food processor; process until finely ground, about 30 seconds. Add remaining ingredients; process until paste-like. Transfer mixture into small saucepan; cook over medium heat 5 to 6 minutes until thickened. Cool.

Mango-Macadamia Filling

Makes 1 cup

½ cup mango preserves
½ cup finely chopped macadamia nuts
2-3 tablespoons sweetened flaked coconut (to taste)
1 teaspoon rum extract

Combine ingredients in bowl. If needed, microwave 10 to 15 seconds to improve spreading consistency. Pineapple preserves or combination of mango and pineapple are also winning flavors.

Orange-Pecan Filling

Makes 1 cup

½ cup firmly packed raisins
½ cup granulated sugar
½ cup freshly squeezed orange juice
2 tablespoons cornstarch
1 teaspoon freshly grated orange zest
½ cup finely chopped pecans

Combine raisins and sugar in bowl of food processor; process 30 seconds or until well blended. Combine raisin mixture, orange juice, cornstarch, and orange zest in small saucepan; cook over medium low heat 5 to 6 minutes until slightly thickened, stirring constantly. Remove from heat and add pecans. Cool. Filling thickens as it cools.

Raspberry-Apricot Filling

Makes 1 cup

⅓ cup <u>seedless</u> raspberry preserves
⅓ cup apricot preserves
¼ cup finely chopped hazelnuts (filberts)
¼ cup sweetened flaked coconut
½ teaspoon ground cinnamon

Combine ingredients in bowl. If needed, microwave filling 10 to 15 seconds to improve spreading consistency.

Sandwich and Layer Fillings

Caramel Crème Filling

Makes ⅔ cup, enough to top an 8-inch pan of brownies

16 light-colored vanilla caramels, unwrapped
⅓ cup sweetened condensed milk
2 tablespoons unsalted butter

Combine ingredients in microwave-safe bowl; microwave, uncovered, on High (100 percent power) 1 minute, or until melted and smooth. Stir after 30 seconds. If necessary, microwave at additional 10 to 15 seconds intervals until melted. Do not overcook.

Cherry Crème Filling

Makes ½ cup

3 tablespoons unsalted butter
¾ cup confectioners' sugar
⅓ cup marshmallow crème
1 teaspoon maraschino cherry juice
2 tablespoons finely chopped maraschino cherries
1 drop red food color

Beat butter and confectioners' sugar with handheld electric mixer until well blended. Beat in remaining ingredients until smooth and creamy. Cover and refrigerate until firm enough to spread, about 1 hour.

Chocolate Filling

Makes ⅔ cup

¼ cup milk chocolate chips
¼ cup semisweet chocolate chips
½ cup sweetened condensed milk
Pinch of salt
½ teaspoon pure vanilla extract

Combine ingredients (except vanilla extract) in microwave-safe bowl; microwave, uncovered, on High (100 percent power) in 30 second intervals, or until melted. Stir after each interval. Stir in vanilla.

Marshmallow Crème Filling

Makes ¾ cup

¼ cup unsalted butter
½ cup marshmallow crème
1 cup confectioners' sugar
Dash of salt
1 teaspoon pure vanilla extract (or favorite)
1 teaspoon milk
1 tablespoon unsweetened cocoa powder (optional)

Combine ingredients in bowl; beat with handheld mixer until smooth and creamy. Filling is thick.

Mint Filling

Makes ½ cup

¼ cup unsalted butter
1 cup confectioners' sugar
1½ teaspoons half and half (or milk)
2 drops green food color
¼ teaspoon pure mint extract

Combine ingredients in bowl; beat with handheld electric mixer until smooth and creamy.

Mocha Filling

Makes ¾ cup

¼ cup unsalted butter
3 tablespoons cream cheese
1¼ cups confectioners' sugar
1 teaspoon boiling water
1 tablespoon <u>instant</u> coffee powder
1 teaspoon pure vanilla extract

Beat butter and cream cheese with handheld electric mixer until well-blended. In small bowl, mix boiling water, coffee and extract; pour it into butter mixture and beat until smooth and creamy.

Oreo® Cream-like Filling

Makes 1 cup

2 cups confectioners' sugar
2 teaspoons pure vanilla extract*
¼ cup solid vegetable shortening
2 tablespoons boiling water

Combine ingredients in bowl; beat with handheld electric mixer until smooth and creamy. Filling is thick.

*Or favorite extract

Peanut Butter Filling

Makes ½ cup

1½ tablespoons water
¼ cup firmly packed brown sugar
1 teaspoon dark corn syrup
¼ teaspoon caramel flavoring (Resources page 164)
¼ cup creamy peanut butter
¼ cup marshmallow crème

Combine water, brown sugar and dark corn syrup in microwave-safe bowl; microwave, uncovered, on High (100 percent power) 1 minute, or until sugar is dissolved. Stir after 30 seconds. Remove from microwave; stir in remaining ingredients.

Peanut Butter-White Chocolate Mousse Filling

Makes 1 cup

1 tablespoon <u>instant</u> white chocolate pudding/pie filling mix or favorite pudding
3 tablespoons milk
⅓ cup unsalted butter
¼ cup creamy peanut butter
1 cup confectioners' sugar
Dash of ground cinnamon
¼ teaspoon pure vanilla extract

Combine dry pudding mix and milk in small bowl; refrigerate 5 minutes. In another bowl, beat remaining ingredients with handheld electric mixer until smooth. Beat in pudding. Refrigerate 15 minutes before using.

Raspberry Crème Filling

Makes ½ cup

3 tablespoons unsalted butter
½ cup confectioners' sugar
⅛ teaspoon salt
⅓ cup marshmallow crème
2 teaspoons <u>seedless</u> raspberry preserves
1½ teaspoons raspberry syrup (such as Torani® Raspberry Syrup)
1 drop red food color

Beat butter and confectioners' sugar with handheld electric mixer until well-blended. Beat in remaining ingredients until smooth. Refrigerate till firm enough to spread.

Fantastic Frostings & Glazes

How do you make an ordinary cookie extraordinary? Frost it!

Some recipes use frostings to intensify and pyramid flavors in the cookie; others add extra sweetness or visual appeal. Frostings are optional but consider the lip-smacking taste value they provide. Experiment with different frostings on your favorite cookies and be pleasantly surprised. **For creamy frostings, have all ingredients at room temperature.**

Jazz up your favorite frostings by changing flavors and textures. To the basic recipe, add assorted spices; finely chopped flavored nuts; candies; dried fruit; jams; sugar-free gelatins; scented sugars; liqueurs such as Amaretto, Kahlua or Grand Marnier; unsweetened cocoa powder; freshly grated citrus zest; or flavored instant coffee diluted in a little water. The possibilities are endless.

If time is an issue, purchase gluten-free frostings and enliven them. Peanut butter added to chocolate frosting or ground cinnamon added to white frosting are two easy ways to dress up store-bought, gluten-free frostings.

Basic Vanilla Cream Cheese Frosting

Makes 1 cup

¼ cup (½ stick) unsalted butter
3 ounces cream cheese
1 teaspoon pure vanilla extract

1½ cups confectioners' sugar
1 tablespoon milk

Beat butter and cream cheese with handheld mixer 1 minute, or until light and fluffy. Beat in remaining ingredients until creamy. If thinner consistency is desired, add more milk.

Variations:

Cranberry Cream Cheese Frosting: Replace milk with freshly squeezed orange juice. Add 2 tablespoons finely cut dried cranberries, 2 tablespoons finely chopped pecans and 1 teaspoon freshly grated orange zest.

Lemon Cream Cheese Frosting: Replace milk and vanilla extract with freshly squeezed lemon juice and lemon or almond extract. Add 1 teaspoon freshly grated lemon zest.

Orange Cream Cheese Frosting: Replace milk and vanilla extract with freshly squeezed orange juice and orange extract. Add 1 teaspoon freshly grated orange zest.

Peanut Butter Cream Cheese Frosting: Replace butter and vanilla extract with creamy peanut butter and caramel extract. Optional: intensify peanut butter flavor by adding ¼ cup chopped peanuts.

Pineapple Cream Cheese Frosting: Replace milk and vanilla extract with pineapple juice and rum extract. Add ¼ cup toasted chopped walnuts or macadamia nuts.

Pumpkin Cream Cheese Frosting: Omit vanilla extract and milk; add 1 tablespoon pure pumpkin and ¼ teaspoon ground cinnamon (Find 100% pure pumpkin in baking aisle).

Basic Buttercream Frosting

Makes 1 cup

¼ cup unsalted butter
⅛ teaspoon salt
½ teaspoon pure vanilla extract

1½ cups sifted confectioners' sugar
1½ tablespoons light corn syrup
1½ tablespoons milk

Beat butter with handheld mixer 1 minute, or until light and fluffy. Beat in remaining ingredients until creamy.

Variations:

Almond Buttercream Frosting: Replace vanilla extract with pure almond extract

Anise Buttercream Frosting: Add ½-1 teaspoon ground anise (to taste)

Chocolate Buttercream Frosting: Add ¼ cup unsweetened cocoa powder and ⅛ teaspoon ground cinnamon

Caramel Frosting

Makes ⅓ cup

2 tablespoons unsalted butter, melted
¼ cup firmly packed light brown sugar
1 tablespoon milk
½ cup confectioners' sugar
¼ teaspoon pure vanilla extract
1-2 teaspoons boiling water (if needed for consistency)

Combine butter and brown sugar in microwave-safe bowl; microwave, uncovered, on High (100 percent power) 30 seconds, or until sugar is dissolved. Stir in milk. Microwave additional 30 seconds; stir. Remove from microwave; beat in confectioners' sugar and vanilla with handheld mixer until smooth and creamy. If frosting becomes too stiff, stir in boiling water, 1 teaspoon at a time until desired consistency is reached.

Fudge Frosting

Makes 1 cup

¼ cup (½ stick) unsalted butter
1½ tablespoons unsweetened cocoa powder
3 tablespoons milk
2 cups confectioners' sugar
½ teaspoon pure vanilla extract
3 tablespoons chopped pecans (optional)
3 tablespoons sweetened flaked coconut (optional)

Put butter, cocoa powder and milk in 2-quart saucepan. Cook, stirring constantly, over medium heat until mixture boils. Remove from heat; beat in confectioners' sugar and vanilla with handheld mixer until creamy. Stir in nuts and coconut, if desired. Spread over hot brownies. Use leftovers as ice cream topping or eat directly out of the bowl!

Maple Frosting

Makes 1 cup

3 tablespoons unsalted butter
3 tablespoons milk
¼ cup pure maple syrup
½ teaspoon maple extract
2 cups confectioners' sugar
¼ cup finely chopped walnuts (optional)

Cook butter in small saucepan over medium heat until brown, 4 to 5 minutes. Stir often. Watch closely; butter burns quickly and can turn bitter. Remove from heat. Beat in milk, maple syrup, maple extract and confectioners' sugar with handheld electric mixer until creamy. Stir in nuts, if desired.

Chocolate Glaze

Makes ½ cup

1 (1-oz.) square unsweetened chocolate, coarsely chopped
1 (1-oz.) square semisweet chocolate, coarsely chopped
2 teaspoons unsalted butter
⅔ cup confectioners' sugar
2 tablespoons boiling water
Pinch of salt
2 teaspoons dark corn syrup
½ teaspoon pure vanilla extract

Combine chocolate pieces and butter in microwave-safe container; microwave, uncovered, on High (100 percent power) in 30 second intervals, or until melted. Stir vigorously after each interval. Stir in confectioners' sugar and boiling water. Stir in remaining ingredients until smooth and creamy. If glaze becomes too stiff, stir in additional boiling water, one teaspoon at a time until desired consistency is reached.

Variations:

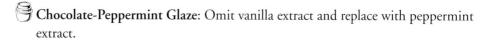**Chocolate-Peppermint Glaze**: Omit vanilla extract and replace with peppermint extract.

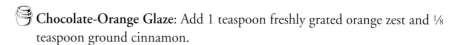**Chocolate-Orange Glaze**: Add 1 teaspoon freshly grated orange zest and ⅛ teaspoon ground cinnamon.

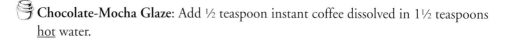**Chocolate-Mocha Glaze**: Add ½ teaspoon instant coffee dissolved in 1½ teaspoons hot water.

Double Chip Glaze

Makes ⅔ cup

½ cup semisweet chocolate chips   ¼ cup unsalted butter
½ cup butterscotch chips*

Put ingredients in microwave-safe container; microwave, uncovered, on High (100 percent power) 30 seconds, or until melted. *Read labels, not all butterscotch chips are gluten-free.

Vanilla Glaze

Makes almost ½ cup

1 cup confectioners' sugar
2 tablespoons milk

1½ teaspoons light corn syrup
½ teaspoon pure vanilla extract

Mix ingredients in bowl with spoon. To add extra richness, stir in 1 tablespoon unsalted butter.

Variations:

Lemon Glaze: Omit milk and vanilla; replace with freshly squeezed lemon juice (hot), ½-1 teaspoon freshly grated lemon zest and ¼ teaspoon lemon oil or ½ teaspoon lemon extract

Lime Glaze: Omit milk and vanilla; replace with freshly squeezed lime juice (hot), ½ -1 teaspoon freshly grated lime zest and ¼ teaspoon lime oil, if desired.

Orange Glaze: Omit milk and vanilla; replace with freshly squeezed orange juice (hot), ½ -1 teaspoon freshly grated orange zest and ⅛ teaspoon ground cinnamon.

Bonus Recipes

Here are a few bonus recipes that you're sure to love.

Delicious and better than their wheat counterpart are comments given about these light tasting **Fabulous Waffles**. Enjoy them as a meal or use them to make an interesting cookie crust as I did in Rocky Road Waffle Bars (page 42).

Great Granola has become the hallmark ingredient in my famous, always requested Grip It & Rip It Granola Bars (page 102) and Crunchy Kiss-A-Roos (page 99). Enjoy granola as a snack, sprinkle it over yogurt or add it to your favorite cereal. You'll be nutritiously satisfied and pleasantly surprised by the wholesome flavorful taste.

The grand finale is **Jack's Homemade Vanilla Ice Cream**. Be prepared to receive high praise when you serve it. It's the blue ribbon winner among our family and friends, especially when served with homemade gluten-free cookies!

Fabulous Waffles	148
Great Granola	149
Jack's Homemade Vanilla Ice Cream	150

Fabulous Waffles

Makes 20 (4 x 4¼-inch) waffles

1½ cups The GF Cookie Lady's Flour (page 4)
1½ teaspoons baking soda
1 teaspoon baking powder

3 large eggs, separated into whites and yolks
1 cup buttermilk
½ cup canola oil
½ teaspoon pure vanilla extract

Preheat waffle iron. Sift flour, baking soda and baking powder; stir. In stainless steel bowl, beat egg whites with electric mixer until soft peaks form, about 30 seconds. In another bowl, combine buttermilk, oil, egg yolks and vanilla; stir in flour mixture. Gently fold in egg whites. Spray waffle iron with vegetable cooking spray. Pour batter (about ¼ cup depending on size of waffle grid). Bake until golden brown. Freeze leftovers in resealable plastic bag, layered between strips of waxed paper, up to 2 weeks.

Tips:

 Eggs (yolks and whites) separate easier when they are cold.

 Whipped egg whites produce greater volume when they are at room temperature.

 Use waffles to make Rocky Road Waffle Bars (page 42).

Variations:

 To enhance flavor and texture, add ground cinnamon, freshly grated nutmeg, chocolate chips or chopped pecans.

Great Granola

Makes 10½ cups

5 cups brown rice crisp cereal
½ cup quinoa flakes
1 cup whole pecans
1 cup raw almonds
1 cup whole walnuts
½ cup salted shelled sunflower seeds
½ cup salted shelled pumpkin seeds (pepitas)
¼ cup sesame seeds
½ cup sweetened flaked coconut (optional)
1 tablespoon flax seed meal
1 teaspoon ground cinnamon

½ cup dark corn syrup
2 teaspoons pure vanilla extract
1 teaspoon pure almond extract
1 tablespoon canola oil

Preheat oven to **300° F.** Set out two (18 x 12 x 1-inch) pans. Do not grease pans.

Combine cereal, quinoa flakes, pecans, almonds, walnuts, sunflower, pumpkin and sesame seeds, coconut, flax seed meal and cinnamon in large bowl. In small bowl, combine dark corn syrup, vanilla, almond extract and oil. Pour syrup mixture over cereal mixture; stir until well coated. Spread mixture evenly between pans. Place both pans in oven at same time. Bake **45 minutes**, stirring every 15 minutes. Spread mixture on waxed paper to cool completely. Store granola in airtight container up to 10 days or freeze for longer storage.

Tips:

 Find brown rice crisp cereal, quinoa flakes and flax seed meal in health food stores.

 If eliminating coconut, add ½ cup favorite nuts.

Variations:

 For nutritional value, replace corn syrup with pure maple syrup, honey or agave nectar. Find agave nectar in health food stores.

Jack's Homemade Vanilla Ice Cream

Makes 1 gallon

6 large eggs
2½ cups granulated sugar
2 quarts half-and-half
½ pint (1 cup) heavy cream
1 (3.4 oz.) box <u>instant</u> vanilla pudding/pie filling
¼ teaspoon salt
2 tablespoons pure vanilla extract

Beat eggs on medium speed until light, about 1 minute. Gradually beat in sugar until thick, about 1 minute. Beat in remaining ingredients. Refrigerate mixture 2 hours or overnight. Freeze in 5-quart ice cream freezer. Follow manufacturer's freezing directions.

Tip:

 Add vanilla powder (Resources, page 162) to further enhance the vanilla flavor. Amount is determined by your tastebuds.

Variations:

 Substitute with your favorite instant pudding mix and extracts.

Techniques

In this section, I invite you to become a "smart cookie" and develop a cookie-cutter mentality. Here you can learn a few baking tricks and common solutions for gluten-free cookie making and baking problems. You don't need to toss your cookies; be a smart cookie and make your baking experience easier, more convenient and with greater success.

Don't forget to check out the equivalent charts. These charts helped me simplify the cookie-baking process. I hope you find them useful too.

Top Ten Cookie-Baking Tricks 152
Equivalent Charts 154
Cookie Troubleshooting Guide 155

Top Ten Cookie-Baking Tricks

Measure now and bake later.
Make cookie mixes in advance by pre-measuring the dry ingredients (gluten-free flours, xanthan gum, spices, leavening agents, salt, etc.). Store in individual resealable plastic bags; label and date each package for personal baking convenience or gift-giving opportunities. Surprise a friend and give a cookie mix. Attach the recipe and write a note such as: "It's gluten-free cookie time, any time you want. Enjoy!"

Save money on unsalted butter.
Most of my cookie recipes call for ¼ cup of unsalted butter with a few calling for ½ cup. Save money and purchase unsalted butter in bulk, such as three-1 pound boxes found in grocery supply stores. Cut the butter slabs into ¼ cup increments, individually wrap in plastic and store in refrigerator up to 1 week or put wrapped portions into a large plastic bag, label and date, and freeze up to 3 months. When you are ready to bake, the butter is pre-measured.

Forgot what ingredients you added?
Place all necessary ingredients on countertop before starting to bake. Set all of the ingredients on the right side of your work area. As you use each ingredient, transfer it to the left side of your work area. That way, if you're interrupted, you can remember which items you have already used and which ones need to be added.

Make half a cookie recipe to see if you like it.
Divide the ingredients in half. If recipe calls for one egg, break the egg into a dish and beat lightly with fork. One large egg equals 4 tablespoons. Use half the beaten egg (or 2 tablespoons) for a half recipe. The trick in measuring the slippery egg mixture is to pour it into a "2 tablespoon" measuring spoon or a 1/8 measuring cup, such as a coffee measuring cup. This measuring spoon is found at kitchen specialty shops and is sold in a set of three along with a 1½ tablespoon and a 2 teaspoon. **Note:** It is difficult to pour egg mixture into a tablespoon, use suggested tool.

Mix now, refrigerate or freeze and bake later.
Most cookie dough can be refrigerated up to 3 days or frozen up to 2 months. Place dough in airtight container, label and date. Thaw dough in refrigerator until it's just soft enough to use.

Other freezing methods:
Freeze individual mounds of dough on cookie sheet; when dough is frozen, place individual pieces in a resealable plastic bag. Or form dough into a log shape, wrap in plastic wrap or aluminum foil and place in resealable plastic bag. Label and date each package. To bake, place frozen mounds or slices of dough on cookie sheet and follow recipe directions. Baking time may need to be increased. **Note:** Do not freeze meringue or any other cookie dough using whipped egg whites because egg whites break down during freezing and cookies will not bake properly.

Chill rolled and filled cookies before baking.
Shape dough into log roll and chill. Slice dough into uniform sizes, place on prepared cookie sheet and refrigerate again before baking. The cookies will hold their shape better.

When melting butter for bottom crust:
It is important that the butter be cooled before adding the remaining ingredients or the mixture will be too oily and the crust may be soggy.

Check the expiration dates on your baking powder and baking soda.
These products start to weaken after 6 months. Expired leavenings produce flat and dense cookies. To determine if chemical leavenings are still active, perform these tests:

Baking powder test: Stir 1 teaspoon baking powder into ½ cup hot water. If there is an immediate fizz, the powder is fine. If not, discard and buy new can. **Note:** Baking powder produces lighter-colored and puffier cookies.

Baking soda test: Stir 1 teaspoon baking soda into ¼ cup of vinegar and check for the fizz. It should froth. If not, put box in the refrigerator to absorb odors and buy a new box for baking purposes. **Note:** Baking soda makes cookies spread and brown more.

Change the flavors of cookies.
Start with your favorite cookie recipe and simply add different spices, herbs, flavoring agents, or different nuts, dried fruit or candy. You'll be surprised with the variety of cookies you can create with a good recipe.

Equivalent Charts

Measurement Equivalent

Dry Measurements	Liquid Measurements
Dash = ⅛ teaspoon or less	1 tablespoon = ½ ounce
1 teaspoon = ⅓ tablespoon	2 tablespoons = 1 ounce
1½ teaspoons = ½ tablespoon	¼ cup = 2 ounces
3 teaspoons = 1 tablespoon	½ cup = 4 ounces
2 tablespoons = ⅛ cup	⅙ cup = 6 ounces
4 tablespoons = ¼ cup	1 cup = 8 ounces
5½ tablespoons = ⅓ cup	2 cups (1 pint) = 16 ounces
8 tablespoons = ½ cup	
10½ tablespoons = ⅔ cup	
12 tablespoons = ¾ cup	
16 tablespoons = 1 cup	

Reducing Ingredients

Original Amount	Half of Recipe	One-Third of Recipe
1 cup	½ cup	⅓ cup
¾ cup	6 tablespoons	¼ cup
⅔ cup	⅓ cup	3 tablespoons plus 1½ teaspoons
½ cup	¼ cup	2 tablespoons plus 2 teaspoons
⅓ cup	2 tablespoons plus 2 teaspoons	1 tablespoons plus 2¼ teaspoons
¼ cup	2 tablespoons	1 tablespoon plus 1 teaspoon
1 tablespoon	1-½ teaspoons	1 teaspoon
1 teaspoon	½ teaspoon	¼ teaspoon
½ teaspoon	¼ teaspoon	⅛ teaspoon
¼ teaspoon	⅛ teaspoon	dash

Cookie Troubleshooting Guide

Cookie baking is an exact science and subtle changes in a recipe can bring different results. Inferior ingredients or different brands, inaccurate measurements, different mixing techniques, variables in ovens, rack position, different baking equipment and even altitude can affect the outcome of your gluten-free cookies.

Check out my Cookie Troubleshooting Guide, if you have problems during the making and baking of the gluten-free cookies.

1. Problem: Gluten-free dough is too sticky and unworkable.	
Cause:	**Solution:**
1. Not enough gluten-free flour	1. Measure accurately. Stir gluten-free flour mixture in the container; then with proper measuring cup "spoon in and level off" flour.
2. Butter too soft	2. Butter should be at room temperature, not squishy but malleable. It should give gently when pressed but still be somewhat firm. Diet margarines or whipped spreads...not suitable for baking..
3. Dough not thoroughly chilled	3. Cover and refrigerate dough 1-2 hours or until firm.

2. Problem: Gluten-free dough cracks when rolled out or flattened.	
Cause:	**Solution:**
Dough too cold	1. Let dough sit at room temperature until it is malleable (5-10 minutes).
	2. Avoid flattening very cold balls of dough (directly out of the freezer) because they will crack around the edges when baked. Allow dough to thaw in refrigerator.

3. Problem: Gluten-free cookies spread too much.	
Cause:	**Solution:**
1. Butter too soft	1. Butter should be room temperature, not squishy but malleable. If butter is too soft, the dough will not hold its shape. Refrigerate dough to firm it. Or try shortening instead of butter or use half butter/half shortening. Diet margarine or whipped spreads not suitable for baking.
2. Oven temperature too low	2. Preheat oven 15 minutes. Use free-standing oven thermometer to ensure accurate temperature. Bake one "test" cookie before making entire batch.
3. Warm cookie sheet	3. Place dough on cool cookie sheets. Use 2-3 identical cookie sheets, while one is baking, another is cooling and the third one is ready to be placed in oven. For a quick cool-down, place cookie sheet in freezer for a few minutes.
4. Cookie sheet greased too much	4. Line cookie sheet with parchment paper. It reduces spread and promotes even baking.

4. Problem: Gluten-free cookies require more/less baking time than stated in recipe.

Cause:	Solution:
1. Incorrect oven temperature	1. Preheat oven 15 minutes. Use free-standing oven thermometer to check oven accuracy.
2. Dough not uniformly shaped in size or thickness	2. Use spring-released cookie scoops to make uniform size cookies. Bake one "test" cookie to determine baking time for **your** oven.
3. Inferior cookie sheets	3. Best cookie sheets are rimless or one-sided, heavy-gauge aluminum with a dull, light-colored finish.
4. Two cookie sheets in oven at same time	4. Place one sheet at a time in the middle of the oven. Allow 2 inches between cookie sheet and oven walls for even browning.
5. Frequently opening oven door	5. If needed, open and close oven door quickly to regulate temperature. Observe through oven window.
6. Different altitudes/humidity	6. Increase baking temperature by 25 degrees and reduce baking time by 1-2 minutes for higher elevations. Bake one "test" cookie to determine temperature and baking time for **your** environment.

5. Problem: Gluten-free cookies are too brown or dark on bottom.

Cause:	Solution:
1. Cookie sheet too thin or too dark	1. Use light-colored, dull-finished, heavy-gauge aluminum, rimless or one-sided cookie sheets. Inferior bake ware can warp in oven and doesn't conduct heat evenly. Dark sheets absorb more heat and cause the cookies to become too brown. Lining cookie sheet with parchment paper promotes even baking.
2. Rack positioned too low in oven	2. Bake one cookie sheet at a time on middle oven rack.
3. Cookie sheet too large for oven	3. There needs to be 2 inches between cookie sheet and oven walls for heat to evenly circulate.
4. Oven temperature too hot	4. Use free-standing oven thermometer to check oven accuracy. Ovens can vary by 50 degrees.
5. Overbaked	5. Check doneness at minimum time indicated in recipe. Bake one "test" cookie to determine baking time and oven temperature setting in **your** oven before making entire batch.
6. Hot spots in the oven	6. Rotate cookie sheet halfway through baking.

6. Problem: Gluten-free cookies fall apart.

Cause:	Solution:
1. Forgot to add xanthan gum	1. Xanthan gum acts as a binder with other ingredients in gluten-free baking. It is a necessary ingredient.
2. Used diet margarine or whipped spreads	2. Use stick butter (unsalted preferred) or shortening. Diet margarines and whipped spreads are full of air and water which makes them unacceptable for baking.

7. Problem: Gluten-free cookies are dry and hard.

Cause:	Solution:
1. Too much gluten-free flour	1. Measure flour accurately. Stir gluten-free flour mixture in container then with proper measuring cup "spoon in and level off".
2. Brown sugar hard and stale	2. Use fresh, soft, moist brown sugar.
3. Forgot baking powder, if recipe calls for it	3. Follow recipe; check expiration date on can..
4. Excess salt	4. Measure salt using measuring spoon and level off.
5. Too much liquid or not enough fat	5. Use large eggs. Jumbo or extra large eggs may provide too much liquid. Use stick butter or shortening and measure accurately.
6. Dried fruit too dry and hard	6. Soak dried fruit in water (or other liquid) to absorb some moisture so it won't take it from recipe. Drain fruit, pat dry, then stir into dough.
7. Overmixed dough	7. Stop mixing when dough is just mixed.
8. Overbaked	8. Check cookies at the minimal baking time. Bake one "test" cookie to make adjustments for your oven. . The centers should appear slightly underbaked. Cookies continue to bake on the cookie sheet once they are removed from the oven.

8. Problem: Baking in high altitudes (over 3000 feet above sea level).

Cause:	Solution:
As altitude increases, air pressure and humidity decrease, altering the way leavening agents, sweeteners and liquids interact	1. Reduce amount of sugar by 1-2 tablespoons.
	2. If recipe calls for baking powder or baking soda, reduce amount by 1/8 teaspoon.
	3. If dough is dry, add 1 tablespoon milk.
	4. Increase baking temperature by 25 degrees and reduce baking time by 1 to 2 minutes.
	5. Store cookies at room temperature for 1 day less than suggested.
	6. Because of lack of humidity, store GF flours in refrigerator or freezer.

Resources

Today you'll find many resources readily available from books, magazines, websites, DVD's, cooking classes and more, to assist you in living a gluten-free lifestyle. This section has a few of my favorite ones. Start with the national celiac support organizations and through them you will find other reliable sources. This is merely a starting point.

Many of my recipes, cookie tips or variations refer to this section. Listed are a few of my favorites gluten-free baking products and specialty items. Remember this is just a beginning!

National Celiac Support Organizations & More 161

Gluten-Free Baking Products. 162

Specialty Items 164

Your Resources:

National Celiac Support Organizations & More

Celiac Disease Foundation (CDF)
13251 Ventura Blvd Suite # 1
Studio City, CA 91604-1838
(818) 990-2354
www.celiac.org

Celiac Sprue Association/USA, Inc (CSA/USA)
P.O. Box 31700
Omaha, NE 68131-0700
(877) 272-4272 (toll free) or (402) 558-0600
www.csaceliacs.org

Gluten Intolerance Group of North America (GIG)
31214 124th Ave SE
Auburn, WA 98092-3667
(253) 833-6655
www.gluten.net

American Celiac Disease Alliance (ACDA)
(National advocacy organization)
2504 Duxbury Place
Alexandria, VA 22308
(703) 622-3331
www.americanceliac.org

Additional Resources:

Numerous books and websites are also available to help you with your dietary needs. Always check if the information is up-to-date and consider the source. Here are two nationally published magazines I like:

Gluten-Free Living
For subscription, go online
www.glutenfreeliving.com

Living Without
For subscription, go online; or find in health food stores
www.livingwithout.com

Gluten-Free Baking Products

The availability of gluten-free foods and the number of gluten-free manufacturers and online suppliers have grown tremendously. Health food stores and supermarkets are expanding their gluten-free product lines. Check online or telephone numbers listed below to find products, catalogs or nearest store locations. This list is just a beginning.

Authentic Foods™
(800) 806-4737
www.authenticfoods.com

Products: many gluten-free flours and starches, including almond meal/flour, brown rice flour superfine, sweet rice flour superfine, gluten-free flour blends, xanthan gum, vanilla powder and more

Bob's Red Mill®
(800)349-2173
www.bobsredmill.com

Products: full line of gluten-free flours and starches, baking mixes, xanthan gum and more

Ener-G Foods, Inc®
(800) 331-5222
www.ener-g.com

Products: gluten-free flours, baking mixes, xanthan gum, guar gum, gluten-free pretzels and more

Gifts of Nature, Inc
(888) 275-0003
www.giftsofnature.net

Products: certified gluten-free oats, gluten-free flours, pre-packaged gluten-free flour blends and more

Gluten-Free Creations Bakery
(602) 522-0659

www.glutenfreecreations.com

Products: gluten-free flour blends, mixes, baked goods, cereals, pastas and more

Gluten Free Oats®
(307) 754-2058

www.glutenfreeoats.com

Products: certified gluten-free rolled oats

Glutino/ Gluten-Free Pantry
(800) 291-8386

www.glutino.com

Products: many gluten-free prepared items including pretzels, baked goods, mixes, pasta, cereals and more

Heartland Ingredients LLC
(888) 658-8909

www.heartlandsfinest.com

Products: navy bean flour, gluten-free flour blend, cereals, pasta and more

PrOatina®
Great Northern Growers,
Montana Producer Cooperative
Carla Dyk, distributor
(406) 284-3362
www.greatnortherngrowers.com

Products: certified gluten-free rolled oats and flour

Specialty Items

The following listings are not gluten-free companies but carry many items that enhance the flavor of gluten-free cookies.

Boyajian, Inc.
(800) 965-0665
www.boyajianinc.com
Products: gourmet pure citrus oils (lemon, lime and orange) and more

LorAnn Oils, Inc
(888) 456-7266
www.lorannoils.com
Products: over 75 super strength flavorings, extracts and more

Nuts 4 U
(800) 688-7482
www.nuts4u.com
Products: nuts, nut pieces, nut flours and dried fruits

Penzeys Spices
(800) 741-7787
www.penzeys.com
Products: quality spices, herbs, extracts, Madagascar vanilla beans and more

Index

A

All About Nuts 121 - 128
    How to Toast Nuts 122
    How to Skin Nuts 123
    How to Make Nut Flours 123
    How to Make Nut Butters 124
    How to Make Almond Paste 126
    How to Make Flavored Nuts 127
All-Time Classic Favorites 13 - 23
    Chocolate Chip Cookies 15
    Magical Macaroons 16
    Oatmeal-Raisin Cookies 17
    Peanut Butter Cookies 18
    PB & Oatmeal-Raisin Chipsters 19
    Snickerdoodles 20
    Spicy Molasses Cookies 21
    Spritz Cookies 22
    Sugar Cookies 23
Almond Butter 124
Almond Buttercream Frosting 143
Almond Paste 126
Almond-Coconut Cups 82
Almond-Toffee Temptations 81
Ambrosia Cookies 63
Anise Aces 64
Anise Buttercream Frosting 143
Apple-Raisin Filling 134
Apricot-Almond Bars 27
Apricot-Coconut Filling 134

B

Banana Mashies 65
Basic Buttercream Frosting 143
Basic Vanilla Cream Cheese Frosting 142
Best-Ever Bars and Brownies 25 - 45
    Apricot-Almond Bars 27
    Brownie Double-Deckers 28
    Candy Bar Brownies 30
    Caramel-Toffee Brownies 31
    Cherry-Almond Cheesecake Bars 32
    CranNutty Bars 33
    Date-Pecan Bars 34
    Frosted Cocoa Brownies 35
    Fudgy Walnut Brownies 36
    Lemon Squares 37
    Peanut Butter Brownies 38
    Pecan Pie Bars 39
    Pumpkin Pie Squares 40
    Raspberry-Marshmallow Brownies 41
    Rocky Road Waffle Bars 42
    Tropical Parfait Bars 43
    Ultimate Peanut-Marshmallow Bars 44
Brownie Double-Deckers 28

C

Candy Bar Brownies 30
Caramel Crème Filling 137
Caramel Frosting 143
Caramel Nut Clusters 95
Caramel-Cashew Cookies 83
Caramel-Toffee Brownies 31
Carrot Cake Cookies 66
Cashew-Almond Butter 124
Cherry Almond Paste 126
Cherry Crème Filling 137
Cherry-Almond Cheesecake Bars 32
Cherry-Almond Filling 135
Cherry-Chocolate Chews 49
Cherry-Raisin Filling 135
Chocolate Buttercream Frosting 143
Chocolate Chip Cookies 15
Chocolate Chip Pralines 50
Chocolate Crème-Filled Miniwiches 51
Chocolate Dynabites 96
Chocolate Filling 137
Chocolate Glaze 145
Chocolate Macaroons 52
Chocolate Roloz 54
Chocolate Surprise Balls 55
Chocolate Waffle Cookies 56

Chocolate-Lover Cookies 47 - 59
    Cherry-Chocolate Chews 49
    Chocolate Chip Pralines 50
    Chocolate Crème-Filled Miniwiches 51
    Chocolate Macaroons 52
    Chocolate-Minty Marvels 53
    Chocolate Roloz 54
    Chocolate Surprise Balls 55
    Chocolate Waffle Cookies 56
    Double Chocolate Delights 57
    Triple Chocolate Bliss 58
    White Chocolate-Macadamia 59
Chocolate-Minty Marvels 53
Chocolate-Mocha Glaze 145
Chocolate-Orange Glaze 145
Chocolate-Peppermint Glaze 145
Cinnabun Swirls 67
Cinnamon Almonds 127
Cinnamon-Almond Butter 124
Citrus Nuts 127
Citrus-Scented Sugar 130
Coconut Mounds 84
Cookie-Baking Tricks 152 - 153
Cranberry Cream Cheese Frosting 142
Cranberry-Pecan Barkie 97
CranNutty Bars 33
Crispy Cappuccino Treats 98
Crunchy Kiss-A-Roos 99

D

Date Cookies 68
Date-Pecan Bars 34
Date-Pecan Filling 135
Double Chip Glaze 145
Double Chocolate Delights 57

E

Equivalent Charts 154

F

Fabulous Fruity 'n Spicy Cookies 61 - 77
    Ambrosia Cookies 63
    Anise Aces 64
    Banana Mashies 65
    Carrot Cake Cookies 66
    Cinnabun Swirls 67
    Date Cookes 68
    Fruit Pizza Cookie 69
    Fruity-Filled Pinwheels 70
    Lemon-Poppy Whiffers 71

    Lime Sugar Cookies 72
    Lime Thumbprints 73
    Pumpkin Cheesecake Cookies 74
    Pumpkin-Chocolate Chip 75
    Strawberry Sensations 76
    Vanilla Sugar-Nutmeg Drops 77
Fabulous Waffles 148
Festive Cookie Wreaths 100
Fillings 133-140
    Apple-Raisin Filling 134
    Apricot-Coconut Filling 134
    Caramel Crème Filling 137
    Cherry Crème Filling 137
    Cherry-Almond Filling 135
    Cherry-Raisin Filling 135
    Chocolate Filling 137
    Date-Pecan Filling 135
    Mango-Macadamia Filling 136
    Marshmallow Crème Filling 138
    Mint Filling 138
    Mocha Filling 138
    Orange-Pecan Filling 136
    Oreo® Cream-like Filling 139
    Peanut Butter Filling 139
    Peanut Butter-White Chocolate Mousse Filling 139
    Raspberry Crème Filling 140
    Raspberry-Apricot Filling 136

Flavored Nuts 127
Flavored Scented Sugars 129 - 132
    Citrus-Scented Sugar 130
    Flower-Scented Sugar 130
    Herb-Scented Sugar 130
    Maple-Scented Sugar 130
    Spice-Scented Sugar 131
    Vanilla-Scented Confectioners' Sugar 131
    Vanilla-Scented Sugar 131
Flower-Scented Sugar 130
Frosted Cocoa Brownies 35
Frostings & Glazes 141 - 146
    Almond Buttercream Frosting 143
    Anise Buttercream Frosting 143
    Basic Buttercream Frosting 143
    Basic Vanilla Cream Cheese Frosting 142
    Caramel Frosting 143
    Chocolate Buttercream Frosting 143
    Chocolate Glaze 145
    Chocolate-Mocha Glaze 145
    Chocolate-Orange Glaze 145
    Chocolate-Peppermint Glaze 145
    Cranberry Cream Cheese Frosting 142
    Double Chip Glaze 145

Fudge Frosting 144
Lemon Cream Cheese Frosting 142
Lemon Glaze 146
Lime Glaze 146
Maple Frosting 144
Orange Cream Cheese Frosting 142
Orange Glaze 146
Peanut Butter Cream Cheese Frosting 142
Pineapple Cream Cheese Frosting 142
Pumpkin Cream Cheese Frosting 142
Vanilla Glaze 146
Fruit Pizza Cookie 69
Fruity-Filled Pinwheels 70
Fudge Frosting 144
Fudgy Fudge Bars 101
Fudgy Walnut Brownies 36

G

Gluten-Free Baking Products 162
Great Granola 149
Grip It & Rip It Granola Bars 102

H

Herb-Scented Sugar 130

I

Intensified Vanilla Extract 132

J

Jack's Homemade Vanilla Ice Cream 150

L

Lacy Almond Cookies 85
Lemon Cream Cheese Frosting 142
Lemon Glaze 146
Lemon Squares 37
Lemon-Pistachio Cookies 86
Lemon-Poppy Whiffers 71
Lime Glaze 146
Lime Sugar Cookies 72
Lime Thumbprints 73

M

Magical Macaroons 16
Mango-Macadamia Cookies 87
Mango-Macadamia Filling 136
Maple Frosting 144

Maple Nuts 128
Maple-Scented Sugar 130
Marshmallow Crème Filling 138
Mint Filling 138
Mocha Filling 138

N

Naturally Nutty Cookies 79, 81 - 91
    Almond-Toffee Temptations 81
    Almond-Coconut Cups 82
    Caramel-Cashew Cookies 83
    Coconut Mounds 84
    Lacy Almond Cookies 85
    Lemon-Pistachio Cookies 86
    Mango-Macadamia Cookies 87
    Orange-Glazed Walnut Cookies 88
    Pistachio-Cranberry Cookies 89
    Spicy Maple Nut 90
    Walnut-Chocolate Chip Biscotti 91
No-Bake, No-Fuss Cookies 93 - 105
    Caramel Nut Clusters 95
    Chocolate Dynabites 96
    Cranberry-Pecan Barkie 97
    Crispy Cappuccino Treats 98
    Crunchy Kiss-A-Roos 99
    Festive Cookie Wreaths 100
    Fudgy Fudge Bars 101
    Grip It & Rip It Granola Bars 102
    Snick-A-Tee Treats 103
    Sweet Nutty Nibbles 104
    White Chocolate-Peanut Crunchers 105
Nut Butters 124

O

Oatmeal-Raisin Cookies 17
Orange Almond Paste 126
Orange Cream Cheese Frosting 142
Orange Glaze 146
Orange-Glazed Walnut Cookies 88
Orange-Pecan Filling 136
Oreo® Cream-like Filling 139

P

PB & Oatmeal-Raisin Chipsters 19
PB&J Jammers 109
Peanut Butter Brownies 38
Peanut Butter Buns 111
Peanut Butter Butterfinger'z 112
Peanut Butter Candy Wedges 113
Peanut Butter Cookies 18

Peanut Butter Cream Cheese Frosting 142
Peanut Butter Filling 139
Peanut Butter Five-Chippers 115
Peanut Butter Lollipops 116
Peanut Butter Monster Cookies 117
Peanut Butter Treasures 118
Peanut Butter-Banana Blasters 110
Peanut Butter-Cran Zingers 114
Peanut Butterlicious Cookies 107, 109 - 118
    PB&J Jammers 109
    Peanut Butter-Banana Blasters 110
    Peanut Butter Buns 111
    Peanut Butter Butterfinger'z 112
    Peanut Butter Candy Wedges 113
    Peanut Butter-Cran Zingers 114
    Peanut Butter Five-Chippers 115
    Peanut Butter Lollipops 116
    Peanut Butter Monster Cookies 117
    Peanut Butter Treasures 118
Peanut Butter-White Chocolate Mousse Filling 139
Pecan Butter 125
Pecan Pie Bars 39
Pineapple Cream Cheese Frosting 142
Pistachio Butter 125
Pistachio-Cranberry Cookies 89
Praline Pecans 128
Pumpkin Cheesecake Cookies 74
Pumpkin Cream Cheese Frosting 142
Pumpkin Pie Squares 40
Pumpkin-Chocolate Chip 75

R

Raspberry Crème Filling 140
Raspberry-Apricot Filling 136
Raspberry-Marshmallow Brownies 41
Resources 161
Rocky Road Waffle Bars 42

S

Sandwich and Layer Fillings 137
Snick-A-Tee Treats 103
Snickerdoodles 20
Specialty Items 164
Spice-Scented Sugar 131
Spicy Maple Nut 90
Spicy Molasses Cookies 21
Spritz Cookies 22
Strawberry Sensations 76
Sugar Cookies 23
Sweet and Spicy Nuts 128
Sweet Fillings 133 - 140
Sweet Nutty Nibbles 104

T

Triple Chocolate Bliss 58
Tropical Parfait Bars 43
Troubleshooting Guide 155 - 157

U

Ultimate Peanut-Marshmallow Bars 44

V

Vanilla Glaze 146
Vanilla Sugar-Nutmeg Drops 77
Vanilla-Scented Confectioners' Sugar 131
Vanilla-Scented Sugar 131

W

Walnut-Chocolate Chip Biscotti 91
White Chocolate-Macadamia 59
White Chocolate-Peanut Crunchers 105